what about the words?

creative journaling for scrapbookers

From the Editors of Memory Makers Books

Denver, Colorado

Managing Editor	MaryJo Regier
Editor	Amy Glander
Art Director	Nick Nyffeler
Graphic Designers	Jordan Kinney, Robin Rozum
Art Acquisitions Editor	Janetta Abucejo Wieneke
Craft Editor	Jodi Amidei
Photographer	Ken Trujillo
Contributing Photographer	Jennifer Reeves
Contributing Writer	Elizabeth Shaffer Harlan
Production Coordinator	Matthew Wagner
Administrative Assistant	Karen Cain
Editorial Support	Kristin Godsey, Emily Curry Hitchingham
Copy Editor	Dena Twinem
Contributing Memory Makers Masters	Amber Baley, Jennifer Bourgeault, Christine Brown, Susan Cyrus, Lisa Dixon, Sheila Doherty, Nic Howard, Julie Johnson, Kelli Noto, Suzy Plantamura, Valerie Salmon, Heidi Schueller, Shannon Taylor, Danielle Thompson, Denise Tucker, Andrea Lyn Vetten-Marley, Sharon Whitehead, Angelia Wigginton, Holle Wiktorek

Memory Makers® What About the Words?

Published by Memory Makers Books, an imprint of F+W Publications, Inc.
12365 Huron Street, Suite 500, Denver, CO 80234
Phone 1-800-254-9124
First edition. Printed in the United States of America.
10 09 08 07 06 5 4 3 2 1

Library of Congress Cataloging-in-Publication Data

What about the words : creative journaling for scrapbookers / from the editors of Memory Makers Books.
p. cm.
ISBN 13: 978-1-892127-77-8
ISBN 10: 1-892127-77-6
1. Photographs--Conservation and restoration. 2. Scrapbook journaling. 3. Scrapbooks. I. Memory Makers Books.

TR465.W49 2006
745.593--dc22

2005058399

Distributed to trade and art markets by
F+W Publications, Inc.
4700 East Galbraith Road, Cincinnati, OH 45236
Phone (800) 289-0963

Distributed in the U.K. and Europe by David & Charles
Brunel House, Newton Abbot, Devon, TQ12 4PU, England
Tel: (+44) 1626 323200, Fax: (+44) 1626 323319
E-mail: mail@davidandcharles.co.uk

Distributed in Canada by Fraser Direct
100 Armstrong Avenue
Georgetown, ON, Canada L7G 5S4
Tel: (905) 877-4411

Distributed in Australia by Capricorn Link
P.O. Box 704, S. Windsor NSW, 2756 Australia
Tel: (02) 4577-3555

what about the words?

My aim is to put down on paper what I see and what I feel in the best and simplest way. —Ernest Hemingway

Scrapbooking is a portrait of our engagement and involvement in life. Simple everyday moments, moments of achievement, moments of solitude, moments of reflection, moments of deep sadness, moments of pure ecstasy—they are all worthy of being recorded in your scrapbook pages. While a picture may be worth a thousand words, it is the journaling—the explanatory text accompanying artwork and photos—that provides the essential backstory. Journaling adds emotional impact in addition to relaying the important details of the events or experiences you are capturing visually through photographs.

But if you're like many scrapbookers, you may approach journaling with trepidation for fear your words will not resonate with the magic and fervor you can so easily infuse into your layout and design. You may worry about the right tone, style or pacing, or you may fear you'll reveal too much information or perhaps too little. *What About the Words? Creative Journaling for Scrapbookers* takes away the fear factor and offers solid advice for turning average anecdotes and day-to-day details into inspired and engaging journaling. You'll find over thirty techniques for formatting your words including letter writing, interviews, words of wisdom, the five senses, lists, poetry, song lyrics and more.

So sit yourself down and allow your inner muse to unleash your creativity. Express through words the full intensity of what you feel and what you've experienced, and your scrapbook pages will echo the true essence of each and every moment.

Sincerely,

Amy

Amy Glander
Editor

Table of Contents

3 just the facts

4 get creative

{borrowed words}

They say imitation is the sincerest form of flattery. It's also one of the easiest ways to begin your scrapbook journaling pursuits if you're experiencing any trepidation from the blank page in front of you. By first immersing yourself in what has been written or spoken by others, you can identify the words and phrases that add emotional texture to the visual biography you are creating. So don't be afraid to borrow words if they perfectly resonate the voice, tone or theme of your scrapbook page. Whether your journaling takes the form of a quote, song or a standard dictionary definition, it's possible that in time these words will help inspire you to find your own inner muse.

1

Play Time

Snack Time

School Time

Sand Time

work Time

AD-INSPIRED

Mosquito Magnet - *Elizabeth White, Clearwater, Florida*

Pick up your local daily and peruse the classifieds or auto section for funky ad-inspired verbiage. Don't discount brochures, fliers, promos, posters and our all-time favorite—the irksome and endless junk mail the postal carrier brings every day without fail. These sources offer a treasure trove of ideas for drafting even the most outrageous, and often hilarious, journaling. Include prices or toll-free numbers for extra pizazz.

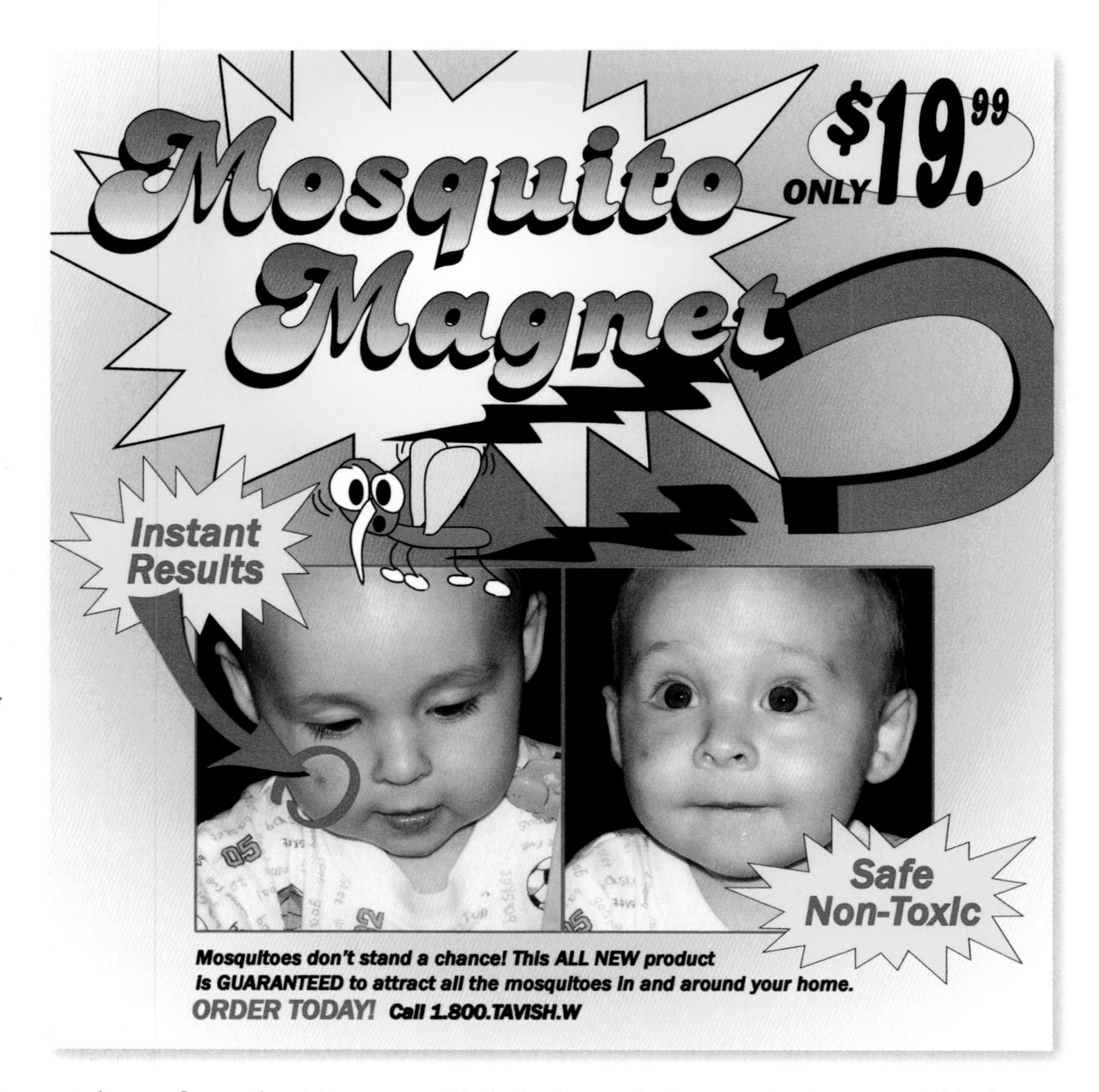

As an art director for an advertising agency, Elizabeth often worked on car advertisements, which she described as "over-the-top and chock-full of starbursts, bright clashing colors and huge price ovals." She spoofed those features for a tongue-in-cheek portrayal of her son's ability to attract mosquitoes. This caricature brings a bit of humor to an unpleasant situation.

SUPPLIES: Image-editing software (Adobe Illustrator, Adobe Photoshop)

Maybe you're one of the lucky ones who can conjure up a catchy phrase or slogan equivalent to that of a professional copywriter for a national ad campaign. But if you're like the rest of us, you're probably inspired by the fetching ads created by others and are happy to play off their ideas to create your own slightly modified version. Radio and TV commercials and print ads in magazines and newspapers offer a wealth of ideas.

After another costly trip to the veterinarian, Susan created this ad-inspired page emulating a well-known credit card campaign. She listed various costs of caring for her dog in contrast to the value of his presence in the family. Her papers mix well with Elliott's fur and the green accents give a dash of whimsy.

SUPPLIES: Patterned papers (Chatterbox); textured cardstock (Bazzill); decorative trim (Offray); jelly label (Making Memories); thread

DEFINITIONS

...In the Eyes of Friends - *Ginger McSwain, Cary, North Carolina*

Create your own definitions written in classic dictionary style to express sentiment that cannot be summed up in a single word. We recommend *Webster's New World College Dictionary* or *The American Heritage College Dictionary* for examples of style and format. You can also find many online reference materials offering language usage and principles at www.bartelby.com.

Ginger created her own definitions to celebrate a wonderful friendship shared by two women. Each block begins with one word in blue and the remaining text in black. This distinction ties the blocks into the rest of the page. She balanced the strength of the striking focal photo with the repetition of the neutral-toned journaling blocks.

SUPPLIES: Patterned papers (Chatterbox); textured cardstock (Bazzill); metal buttons (K & Company); printed twill, ribbon (Michaels, Morex Corp.); staples; silk flower

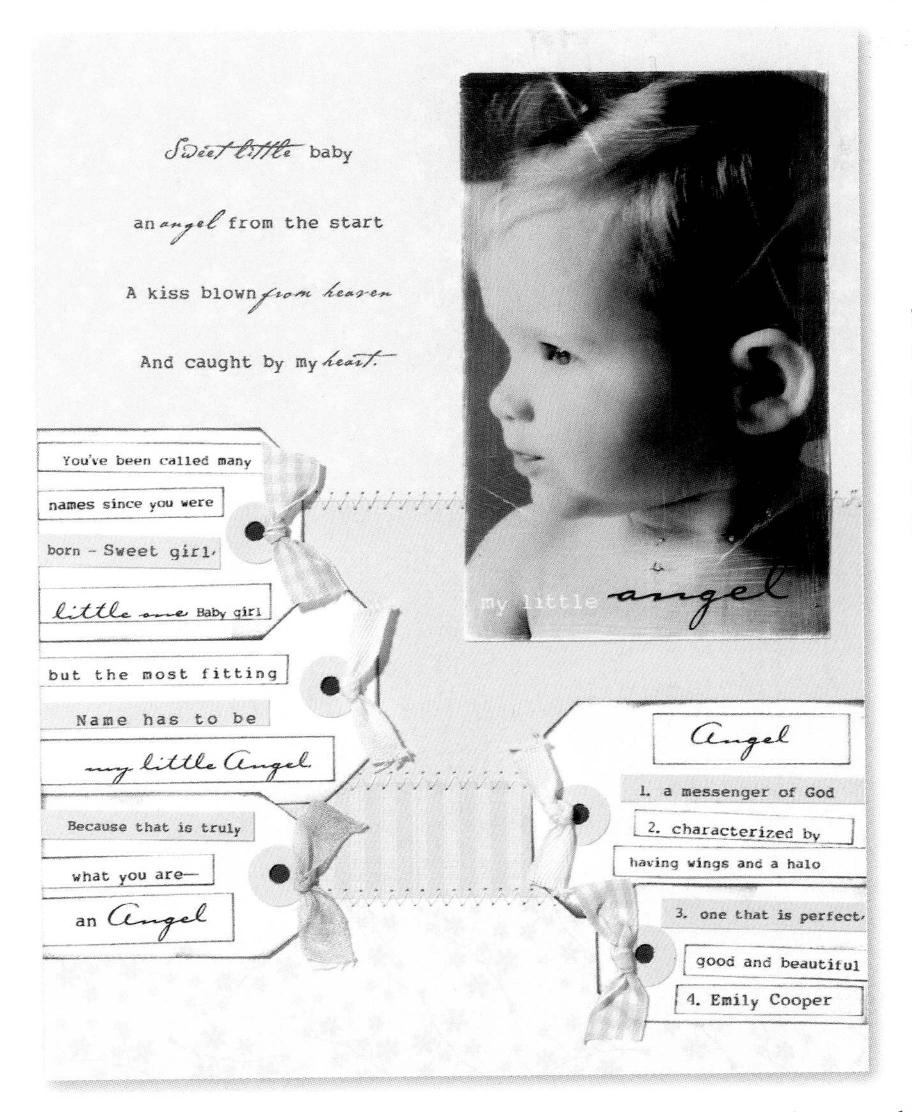

With definitions, you can stick with the classic dictionary varieties, but you can also add spice by incorporating the name of a special person who embodies those characteristics.

Rebecca visited a favorite scrapbooking Web site in search of a definition, but instead found her opening quote. To complete the journaling, she added the definition of "angel," the first three meanings reflecting the formal dictionary version and adding her daughter's name as the fourth to perfectly characterize the word. Her distressed photo and soft color palette give a sweet and tender look to the page.

SUPPLIES: Patterned papers (Chatterbox); angel quote (www.twopeasinabucket.com); image-editing software (Adobe Photoshop); twill (Creative Impressions); ribbons; sandpaper; cardstock; thread; stamping ink

DEFINITIONS

Drool - *Lindsay Jordon-Hegwald, Valley Center, Kansas*

Expand on a standard dictionary entry by adding your own witty commentary to the mix. You'll find that drafting the "definition" in your own voice is fun and easy and will be sure to bring a smile to your readers.

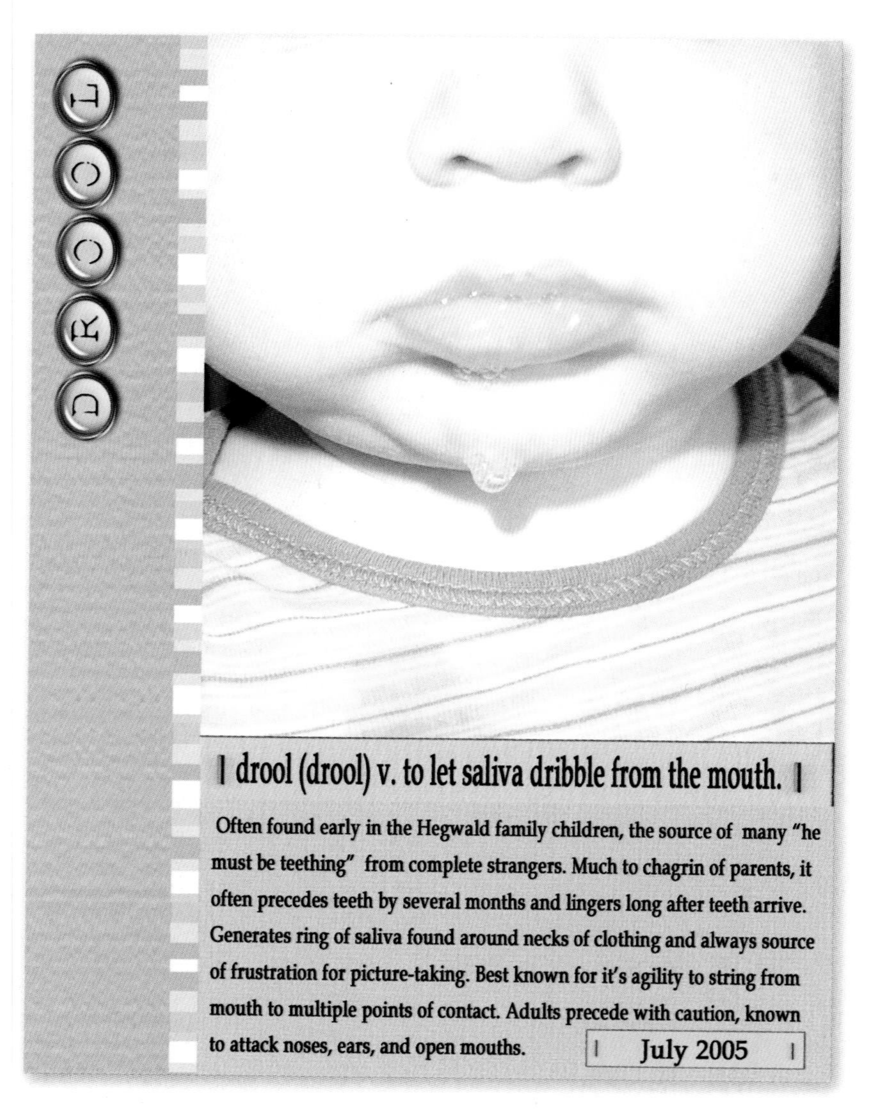

Beginning her journaling with the classic definition of "drool," Lindsay personalized it to include the history of the family's hereditary drooling. She even conveys with plenty of humor the scientific properties of the secretion. She says, "I almost deleted this picture since so much of his face was gone." As time went by, she began to like it, and she created the perfect layout to complement it.

SUPPLIES: Digital kit (Beach Blues Kit, www.digitaldesignessentials.com); image-editing software (Adobe Photoshop Elements 3.0)

Insecure - *Shannon Taylor, Bristol, Tennessee*
Photo: Robert Taylor, Bristol, Tennessee

A dictionary definition is one of the best ways to convey heartfelt sentiments and deep emotion. Straightforward and to the point, a classic dictionary definition gets to the heart of the matter and allows you to express feelings that otherwise may be hard to put into your own words.

By featuring a definition, Shannon set up the mood and theme of her page. She wrote candid journaling describing in depth her feelings of insecurity. Her black-and-white photo is framed by large patterned paper flowers that she hand-trimmed and gave dimension to with foam adhesives. She surrounded the image with a rich, fall color scheme.

Supplies: Patterned papers (Scenic Route Paper Co.); chipboard label holder (Heidi Swapp); plant labels (Weathered Door); rub-on letters (Making Memories); ribbons (Offray); brads; acrylic paint; chalk; cardstocks

Choices - *Jennifer Bourgeault, Macomb Township, Michigan*
Poem: "The Road Not Taken" by Robert Frost

Poetry is the music of the heart. Whether your style is the lyrical musings of Robert Frost or the deep emotion of Sylvia Plath, you can express yourself through the work of poets the world over. Whether you borrow words from the Bible or more contemporary poets, poetry can be a great way to capture sentiments you cannot express in your own words.

Beginning with one of her favorite poems, Jennifer created a page for her son. After placing the poem on the page, she wrote a personal message to him, reminding him about the choices he will have to make and be responsible for during his life. She used traffic images to symbolize the road he will travel.

SUPPLIES: Patterned paper (Daisy D's); circle punch (Creative Memories); chipboard strip (Heidi Swapp); traffic and number stickers (Sticker Studio); plastic embellishment, brad (Junkitz); chalk ink (Clearsnap); flower stamp (Savvy Stamps); cardstocks

Living on the Edge - *Susan Cyrus, Broken Arrow, Oklahoma*
Quote: Anonymous

A quotation, whether from a famous person or your next-door neighbor, can be the perfect touch to make your journaling pop off the page and really speak to your audience. The good news is that with the help of the Internet, quotes are easy to find.

While listening to a radio commercial, Susan heard this quote and knew it would be great on a page. She did some research online to confirm its accuracy and then created a playful page using it as the title. She designed the background paper using image-editing software and added vivid colors that coordinated with the photos. To create more texture on the page, she tore strips off the bottom of the focal photo and added small journaling strips in between.

SUPPLIES: Patterned papers (Carolee's Creations, Creative Imaginations, Karen Foster Design); star punch (EK Success); star conchos (Scrapworks); image-editing software (Adobe Photoshop 7.0)

You're Fired - *Kim Crothers, Ridgeland, Mississippi*

Just turn on your TV and you're likely to hear snappy catchphrases that perfectly summarize a witty sentiment or feeling. Popular TV shows, commercials, tag lines from local businesses or media and popular lingo heard on the street can all be inspiration for scrapbook journaling.

Being fans of a popular television show, Kim's son pointed at her and said, "You're fired!" She chuckled and then created a digital page about the incident. She recalled a small part of the conversation and added other journaling to fill out the story being told. In her image-editing software, Kim enhanced the edges of the photos and the journaling block with a brush technique, giving them a well-worn look.

SUPPLIES: Image-editing software (Adobe Photoshop); background paper (Dirt Paper Pack, www.creativesnaps.com); photo borders (Sloppy Borders Kit, www.creativesnaps.com)

Believe in Boston - *Christa Krupski, Kirksville, Missouri*
Slogan: Boston Red Sox

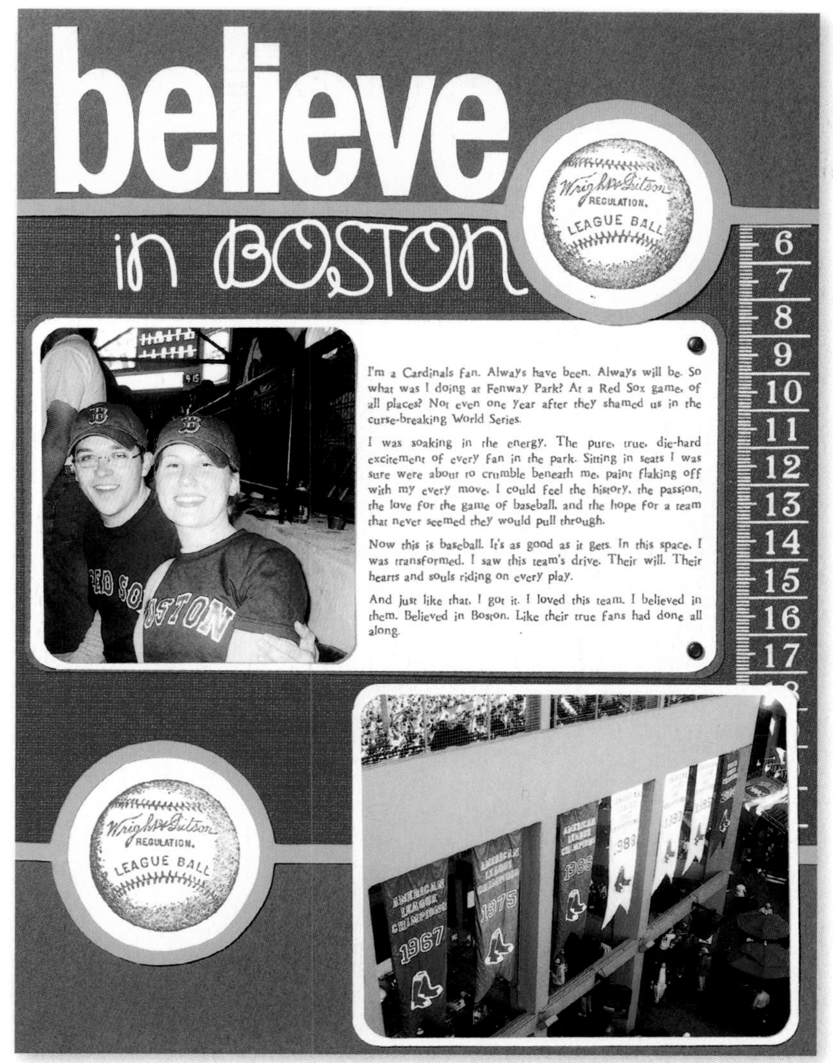

Picked up a catchy phrase or slogan lately? The words are all around you. Find inspiration in the words you encounter in everyday life to create titles and journaling. If the words are particularly galvanizing, you'll be likely to remember them and they'll offer an even stronger impact on your page.

Being a die-hard fan of the St. Louis Cardinals did not negate the feelings that Christa experienced during a Red Sox game at Fenway Park. She wrote about her experience, expressing the impact that the fans, the team and the park had on her. The team's slogan for the 2004 World Series, "Believe in Boston," fit perfectly with her page so she used it as her title and the focus of her journaling.

SUPPLIES: Letter stickers (American Crafts); textured cardstock (Bazzill); baseball stamp (Rubber Cottage); mini brads (Making Memories); Gaffer tape (7 Gypsies); corner rounder (Marvy); stamping ink; cardstock

I Love to Read All Kinds of Books - *Alecia Ackerman Grimm, Atlanta, Georgia*

Add quotes that relate to the topic or theme of your layout. Here the artist chose quotes from famous writers to further display her love for reading.

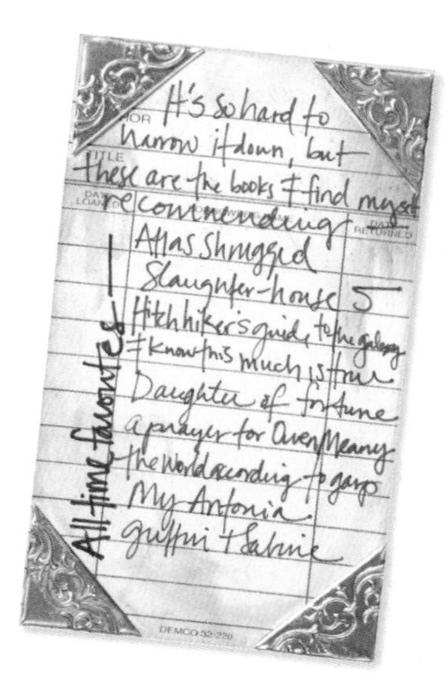

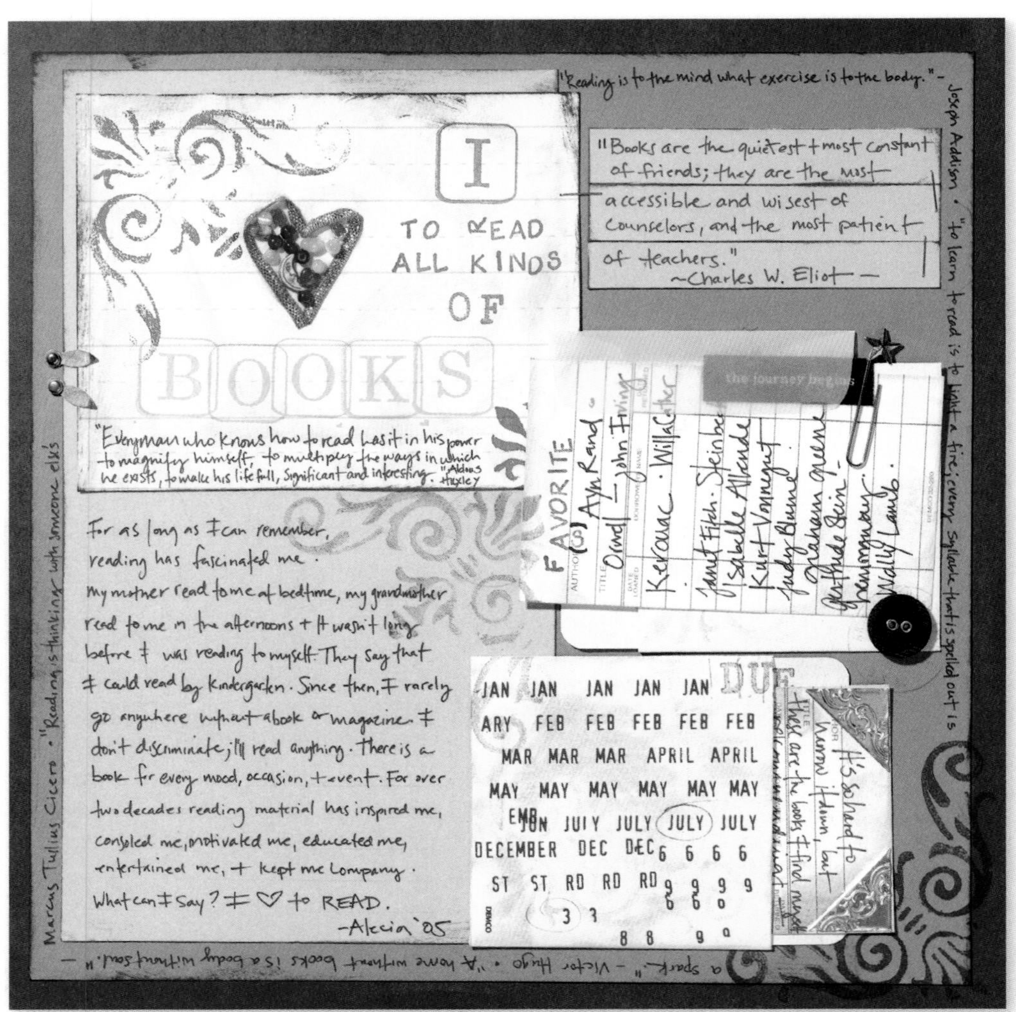

A lover of all things literary, Alecia is no stranger to the written word. She incorporated library cards and envelopes to list her all-time favorite books and authors. The vibrant pink of her handmade heart illustrates her passion in contrast to the various shades of blue reflecting a serious literary tone.

SUPPLIES: Library pocket, cards, envelope (Foundations); decorative paper clip (Nunn Design); foam stamps, photo corners, mini brads (Making Memories); letter stamps (Jo-Ann Stores); distress ink (Ranger); rub-on dates (Autumn Leaves); buttons (Junkitz); woven label (Me & My Big Ideas); dimensional adhesive (JudiKins); ribbon; beads; acrylic paint; pen

PANTONE I4-4II0

heather

"The colors that we see all around us are a reflection of the sun's light in all it's glory. It is magic made visible. There is nothing more miraculous, unexpected or wondrous than seeing a rainbow appear in the sky." – Colorstrology

weblog entry may 17, 2005

I love the quote above (and the folks at Pantone!) - it seems to capture and describe what is undescribable: Color.

Take for example, how do you describe to someone the color green? At first you might think, "well...it's green. Green is green." But what if you were able to describe that same green in other senses? "Green is the color of life. It is the smell of fresh, clean goodness. It is the feel of coolness and the taste of that which grows from this earth."

According to Michelle Bernhardt, just as you were born under a certain sun sign, you too have a personal color that corresponds to the real you.

My personal color is Pantone I4-4II0 Heather.
Description: Realistic. Serious. Funny.

To say the least, this wouldn't be my first choice. It's...too light. Too...wispy. A tad bit too feminine. And to put it like it is...too serious. I like to think of myself as outgoing, fun loving. Shouldn't I be something more...bold? More bright? More cheerful?

Don't be so judgemental at first. As Michelle Berhardt points out, your favorite color is shaped by various experiences and outside influences (I didn't really have a favorite anyway), but your birth color is constant. Perhaps you may be suppressing one aspect of your life, and these traits aren't as prevalent as they are at other times.

Hmmm...food for thought....turns out my personal color does maybe make sense. My color descriptors are very much opposites and complimentry.

And, I do very much have a yin and a yang about me. I'm told a lot that I'm very mature for my 24 year old age. I'm a planner and I'm a spender. I'm a jokester and I'm a sensitive soul.

What I love most of all is the intro to my personal color: "There is a logical and serious side to your nature combined with a wild sense of adventure and childlike wonder."

This should be my personal mantra. It's so....well, ME.

OCTOBER 4

realistic. serious. funny.

Share your personality through symbolism. In this example, the artist chose to use color to represent who she is. She opened and closed her description with quotes that related to the topic she was writing about.

For this page, Amber found inspiration from a Web site that matches colors to personalities. After finding her personal color on the site, she recorded her feelings about the description in narrative form. She used her color, Heather, as a major feature of the page.

SUPPLIES: Image-editing software (Adobe Photoshop); digital photo frame (downloaded from the Internet); quotes and color analysis (www.colorstrology.com)

SONG LYRICS

Boing Curls *- Nora Noll, Glastonbury, Connecticut*
Song Lyrics: adapted from "Peggy Sue" written by Buddy Holly

Is there a jingle or ditty that makes your heart go thump every time you hear it? Perhaps it brings to mind a special someone or re-creates a forgotten memory. A fun way to play with song lyrics is to adapt them to suit the theme or subject of your layout. Choose a tune that is easily recognizable and alter or flip-flop the words to reflect the meaning you are trying to convey.

Life events are often tied to music. A song floats into the heart when something happens, and it becomes a part of that event. When Nora's daughter's hair seemed to curl up overnight, the song "Peggy Sue" sprang to mind. From there, her thoughts landed on the name Curly Sue and she created this page to remember the story. As part of the page, Nora included her own version of the lyrics and her own definition sticker.

SUPPLIES: Patterned papers, letter stickers (Basic Grey); textured cardstock (Bazzill); phrase stickers (Pebbles); ribbon (Morex Corp.)

For Those About to Rock - *Kelli Noto, Centennial, Colorado*
Song Title: "For Those About to Rock (We Salute You)"
written by Ronald Belford Scott (aka Bon Scott) of AC/DC

Song titles are another clever device to borrow when in search of words. You can take words and apply your own special meaning to them. Other types of titles to consider are those from books, films or television shows.

Kelli's son, along with three friends, formed a rock band, and the kids love to work on songs from AC/DC. The title of the song "For Those About to Rock" summed up her theme perfectly and became the title of her layout. She added song titles and popular bands to the journaling to reinforce the theme. Kelli modified the striking focal photo to highlight each player in the band.

SUPPLIES: Patterned papers, monograms (Basic Grey); image-editing software (Adobe Photoshop CS); transparency; acrylic paint; cardstocks

simple starts

Time to loosen your inhibitions, stretch your imagination and send that inner critic on vacation. This chapter presents easy formats for creating tightly written little gems in the form of lists, short phrases, repeated words and numbered steps. These simple starts will punctuate your scrapbook pages with charisma, humor and a whole lot of detail. You'll discover the fun in drafting words and phrases that are short and snappy to cleverly spin your one-of-a-kind tale.

2

Pockets
of
WISDOM
All things go
Learning is a
carried in the pocket.
What you giv
When yo
all your heart.
is always young.
ndow of the soul.
Every path ha
There is
Enjoy yourself.
May your POCKETS be heavy and your HEART be light. May GOOD LUCK Pursue you each morning and night.
-Irish Blessing-
G

SINGLE WORDS

ABC of U - *Carrie Ferrier of Destination Scrapbook Designs, Fort Wayne, Indiana*

We all know our ABCs. A variation of the acrostic style of journaling, using the letters of the alphabet to list personal characteristics is a fun and easy way to share details about an important person in your life.

Carrie created this page about her niece Kristen using stickers from a product line featuring characteristics beginning with many of the letters in the alphabet. She described Kristen's personality by using the stickers in alphabetical order. She created a block of punched patterned papers echoing the colors in her niece's shirt. This, along with the striped patterned papers, adds whimsy, color and flair to the page.

SUPPLIES: Patterned papers, word stickers (Destination Scrapbook Designs); postage-stamp punch (McGill); mini and heart brads; cardstock

A fun way to feature single words is to list them in a compare-and-contrast format. Make a list of personal characteristics, favorites, pet peeves or colloquial speech and then compare them item-by-item with those of a loved one. The results are likely to be entertaining, and it will serve as a great way to document the things that set you apart from one another.

Judith says, "When East Coast meets West Coast, a translator is sometimes required." To capture the everyday words that she and her husband, Dean, say differently, she created a comparative list. To highlight the contrast, she adhered them at different heights on the page. Her design also features contrasts between the photos with vibrant blue shirts set against the muted background tones, as well as a strong presence of circles versus rectangles.

SUPPLIES: Patterned paper, stickers (SEI); tearing ruler (Plaid); cardstocks

Favorites at 1 - *Shaniqua Young, Canton, Georgia*

Mix it up! Shake up journaling labels by mixing action words with nouns and employing a variety of letter treatments such as Dymo labels, rub-on letters, stamped letters and computer fonts. Have fun designing with words and allowing the wealth of lettering options to spark your creativity.

To design a list of her son's favorite activities, Shaniqua combined label maker and cardstock strips. She stamped and used rub-on letters on the cardstock strips and created a fun block by mixing up and adhering the styles. Her choice of soft, earthy tones gives the page a charming, youthful look. Ribbons placed along the side of the page add softness and lead the eye to her title tag.

Supplies: Patterned papers (Basic Grey); letter stamps (Colorbök, EK Success, Hero Arts, Stamp Craft); solvent ink (Tsukineko); rub-on letters (Making Memories); ribbons (All My Memories, Michaels); label maker (Dymo); staples; tag; cardstock

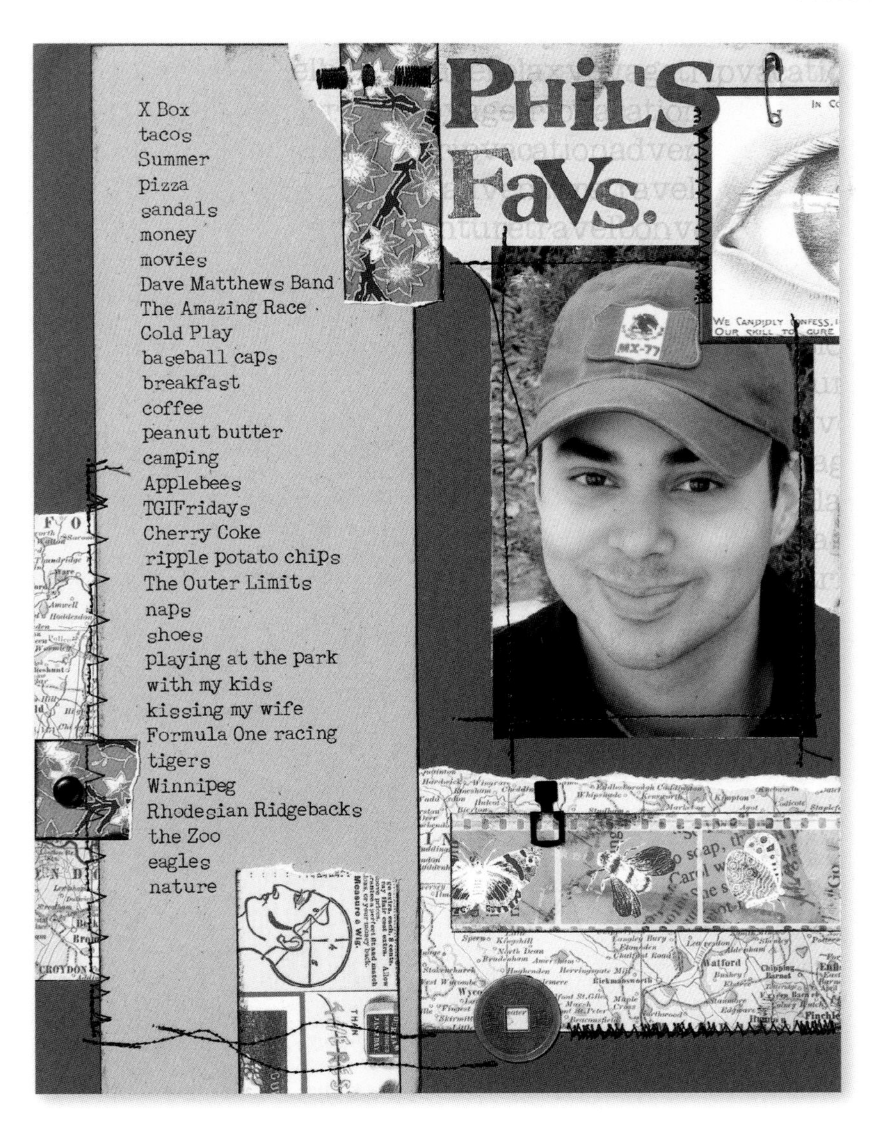

Recording favorites in list format is an easy and straightforward approach for creating a page all about a loved one. There's no better way to create a picture-perfect portrait of that special someone than to record the things he or she loves most. Step it up a notch by asking your subject to jot down his or her much-loved items every year, every five years, etc. It will create a fun exercise for seeing which faves are set in stone and which were mere desires of the day.

With a scrapbook page in mind, Maria asked her husband, Phil, what some of his favorite things were. She says, "I just jotted them down as he rattled off a random list. It was fun but some of the things surprised me." She featured his list in a column form surrounded by artsy papers, images and his photo.

SUPPLIES: Patterned papers (DMD, K & Company, Me & My Big Ideas); letter stickers (Basic Grey); Chinese coin (DMD); metal tab (7 Gypsies); brad (SEI); thread (Coats & Clark); solvent ink (Tsukineko); cardstocks; safety pin

SINGLE WORDS

Intoxicating to all of the Senses - *Suzy Plantamura, Laguna Niguel, California*

Set your writing free by allowing yourself to brainstorm the words that best encapsulate the sensations a setting or experience induce. Use the five senses—sight, sound, smell, touch and taste—as your blueprint to easily structure words or phrases that capture the charisma and emotion and create a mental imprint for your readers who will grow green with envy because they weren't there to experience it with you.

When Suzy traveled to Hawaii, she felt the island envelop all her senses. She used a series of descriptive words paired with both the small photos and the striking panoramic photo to communicate the true essence of what she felt.

Supplies: Patterned paper (NRN Designs); printed ribbon (Making Memories); letter stickers (Sticker Studio); rub-on letters (Me & My Big Ideas); stamping ink

"These are a few of my favorite things..." Documenting a mixture of favorite things is a fun way to profile your or someone else's character. Here the artist chose to add flavor to her list by launching her page with a quote that sums up her theme. She then added plus signs between each noun to give the impression that all the elements added together combine to create her character.

Amber created a list of all the things she loves. The digital papers she chose, along with the funky fonts, reflect her personality as much as the list of simple pleasures. For a special touch, Amber drew a flower, scanned it into image-editing software and added it several times to her photo.

Supplies: Patterned papers and quote (San Diego Digital Kit, www.citrusblossoms.com); image-editing software (Adobe Photoshop); flower brushes (artist's own design)

SINGLE WORDS

My Husband - *Katja Kromann, Mission Viejo, California*

Personal characteristics do not have to be presented in a simple list format. You can write in regular sentences and employ a variety of mediums to highlight the key words.

Katja created this page to honor her husband's talent as a senior software engineer and his humility regarding his accomplishments in the field. She wanted him to know how much she appreciates these qualities and how it has inspired her to work toward a similar attitude. Using just three colors, she created a montage of word textures with tags, strips, labels and frames.

Supplies: Patterned papers (DieCuts with a View, K & Company, Rusty Pickle); embossed papers (K & Company); textured cardstock (Bazzill); rub-on letters, brads, foam letter, decorative corner stamps (Making Memories); label maker (Dymo); letter stickers (Deluxe Designs, Mrs. Grossman's); die-cut tags, mini frames (Accu-Cut); letter frames, metal letter (Deluxe Designs); heart punch (EK Success); ribbons (Michaels, Offray); die-cut flower (Paper House Productions); acrylic paint; paper clips; paper crimper

Mix and match favorites with personal characteristics. By including an assemblage of details, you give your readers a glimpse into the character of the subject at a particular age.

Robin asked a co-worker of hers to write some journaling and she designed the page as a surprise for her. When she wrote the journaling, she included a bevy of characteristics of Dominic at 2 years old, and Robin highlighted them with arrow bullets. She used orange as a dramatic accent to a design that features primarily black-and-white papers and images.

SUPPLIES: Patterned papers, stencil number, vellum quote (Autumn Leaves); date stamp; embroidery floss; stamping ink; pen; cardstocks

Decade Apart - *Kimberly Kesti, Phoenix, Arizona*

Use lists of single words to document the unique differences between siblings, lifelong friends, co-workers, spouses, etc. Items to list can include birth order, age, physical attributes, favorite things to do, grade in school or occupation, personality traits and nicknames.

Two of Kimberly's seven children were born 10 years apart, and their personalities reflect major differences. She featured solo photos of the girls and comparative journaling of their personalities, attitudes and likes. By placing them all inside the focal circle, she kept the focus on the center. She brought the page together with a collection of punched circles bordering the central design.

SUPPLIES: Textured cardstocks (Bazzill); circle punch (EK Success); letter stickers (Memories Complete); brads, photo turns (Junkitz); stamping ink

We Are Your Parents - *Alecia Ackerman Grimm, Atlanta, Georgia*
Photo: Christina Ackermann, Alpharetta, Georgia

Create an interesting design element by recording a montage of thoughts or feelings in a random format on your layout. Allow one statement to flow into the next without overthinking by handwriting your thoughts. This will give your loved ones a wonderful record of your personal handwriting style to cherish forever.

Alecia created this page by placing paper blocks as the foundation and then adding her photos. She designed the title and says, "Once all of that was in place, I started to fill in the blank spaces with journaling." To finish the page, she filled blank spaces with embellishments that supported her theme.

SUPPLIES: Patterned papers (Basic Grey, Scenic Route Paper Co.); label stickers (Pebbles); rub-on letters (KI Memories, Making Memories); decoration stickers (Mustard Moon); rub-on stitching (My Mind's Eye); letter stickers (Scenic Route Paper Co., Sticker Studio); buttons (SEI); acrylic heart and jewels (Heidi Swapp); dimensional adhesive (JudiKins); definition stickers (Making Memories); distress ink (Ranger); chalk ink (Clearsnap); cardstocks; pen

SIMPLE PHRASES

21 Things - *Erin Sweeney, Twinsburg, Ohio*

For a fun writing exercise, sit down and generate a numbered list of the traits or qualities you love and admire in someone. The items can run the gamut from morals and beliefs to laughter and a loving smile. For even more fun, choose fonts that symbolize the feeling or sentiment you are trying to convey. In this example, the artist chose a scripty font to convey hugs and kisses and a funky font to convey lightheartedness and goofy behavior.

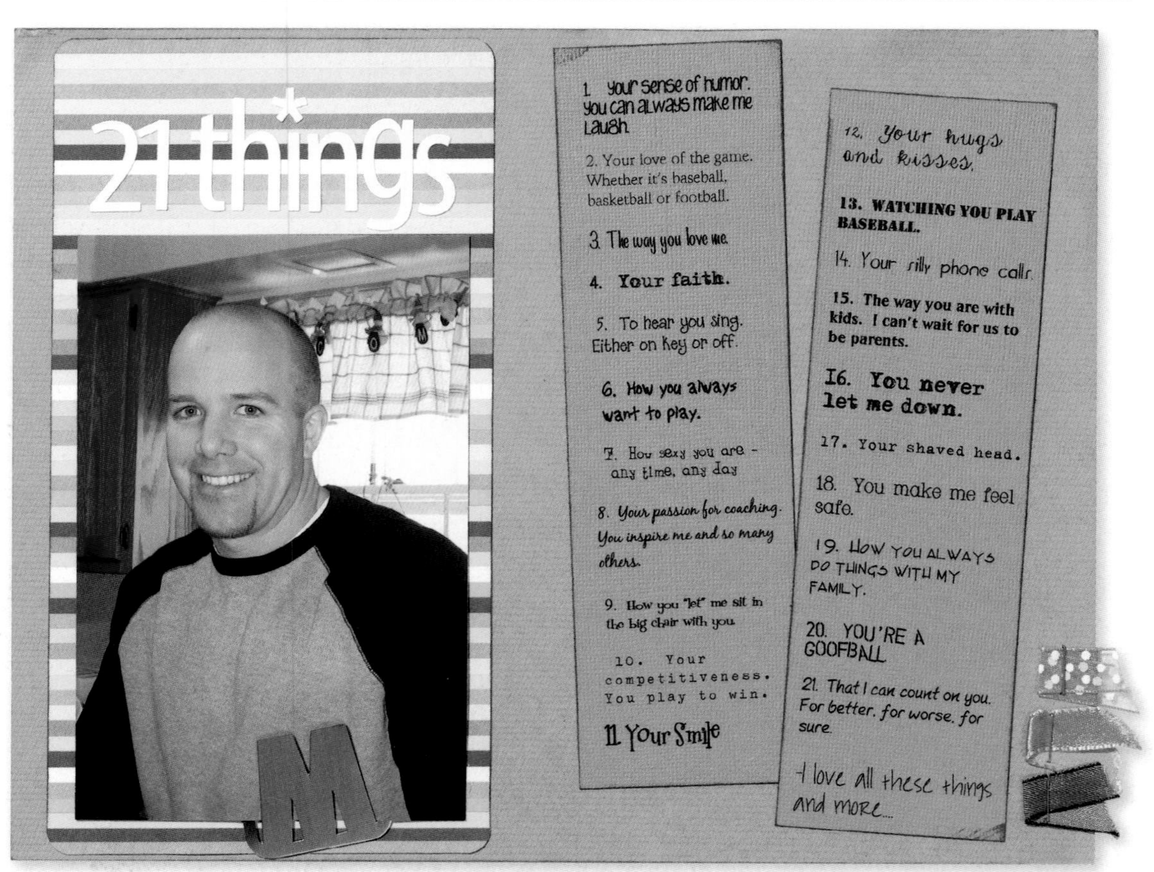

Erin wanted to create a page about all the things she loves about her husband. She felt that creating a list would make the journaling easy to read and would allow her to include the most characteristics. She used 21 different fonts to give the list a fun and funky look. It created such an interesting look that she only added a few embellishments to complete the page.

SUPPLIES: Patterned paper (KI Memories); textured cardstock (Bazzill); letter stickers (Doodlebug Design); metal letter clip (Scrapworks); distress ink (Ranger); ribbons (May Arts, SEI); staples

A great way to document the milestones or highlights of a year is to record them in block format. Choose a birthday, anniversary, the end of a school year, New Year's Eve or any other commemorative or recurring day that ignites reflection and heartfelt contemplation. These can be written as simple sentences or phrases and can share the special moments that are forever engraved in your memory.

Things change so quickly when children are young. Courtney captured the highlights of a year by recording special things that happened. She handwrote each accomplishment on journaling blocks, inked the edges and sprinkled them around the page. To emphasize her daughter's age, she handcut a line of numerals to create a chronological timeline and added a target border around the 3.

SUPPLIES: Patterned papers, letter stickers, rivet, cardstock stickers (Chatterbox); watermark ink (Tsukineko); pen; staples

SIMPLE PHRASES

Things I've Learned Along the Way - *Lilia Meredith, Scottsdale, Arizona*

Journal the lessons you've learned or your perceptions on the stages of life in numbered-list format. Your items can center on one theme such as relationships, parenting or finding your own niche in the world. They can also be a combination of different observations that reflect your personality and the road you've traveled.

Lilia turned a list of witty observations into a fun page about life lessons. She used her own handwriting to add a whimsical touch to her musings. For quick embellishments, she repeated rub-ons and stamped images. Patterned paper flowers cascade down the side of the page for another quick embellishment.

SUPPLIES: Patterned papers (7 Gypsies, KI Memories, Making Memories); decorative tape (Heidi Swapp); solvent ink (Tsukineko); rub-on stitching, flower and number (Autumn Leaves, Heidi Swapp); sun, moon, and number stamps (Stampotique); "original" stamp (source unknown); staples; pen; cardstock

Showcase an inanimate object that brings joy to your family and home. For a fun twist you can include the perspective of the object on short journaling strips. In this example, the artist also chose to share the "activities" of the beloved teddy bear by listing the many ways he brings joy into her daughters' lives.

Jennifer turned short sentences into matted journaling strips. Some of the strips feature feelings in the girls' own words and some are from Jennifer's observations. Each shares a precious memory of Charlie Bear. She created a library pocket to fit extra strips and sprinkled the rest directly on the page.

Supplies: Patterned papers (Colorbök, Junkitz); textured cardstocks (Bazzill); brads (Karen Foster Design, Making Memories); letter buttons (Junkitz); rub-on letters (Making Memories); rub-on stitches (Doodlebug Design); embroidery floss (DMC); ribbons (Doodlebug Design, May Arts); ultra-thick embossing enamel, distress ink (Ranger); die-cut bear (QuicKutz); stencil letter (source unknown); acrylic paint; leather cord; pen; faux suede fabric; stuffing

Remarkable You - *Lisa Cole, Puyallup, Washington*

Personalize a bulleted list by including your own handwriting. List the reasons why you love that special someone.

Lisa loved the silly grin on her daughter's face, and it brought to mind other traits that she adores. Putting those thoughts together inspired her to create a page featuring bits of her daughter's personality. She used a premade sticker tag to handwrite a bulleted list of her favorite attributes. Fresh and feminine colors and embellishments complement her black-and-white photo.

SUPPLIES: Patterned papers (Bo-Bunny Press, Doodlebug Design); sticker tag (Bo-Bunny Press); rub-on and sticker letters (Creative Imaginations, KI Memories, Li'l Davis Designs, Making Memories); spiral paper clip (Clipiola); ribbons (Stampin' Up!); wooden frame (Li'l Davis Designs); paper flower (Making Memories); acrylic letter (Doodlebug Design); diva charm (Michaels); stamping ink; fibers

Let your journaling take on a whole new shape by handwriting or printing it to reflect the contours of the subject or theme you are writing about. This technique requires a bit more planning, but will serve as a perfect portrait for sharing the descriptive details of an experience or event.

To resemble ocean waves crashing onto the shore, Rebecca journaled in a pattern directly onto her background. She sketched the patterns using a faint pencil line and then wrote carefully along the lines using all capital letters. The page is simple yet dramatic: the white gel pen contrasts with the black background and with a burst of hot color from the letter stickers.

Supplies: Letter stickers (Imagination Project); textured cardstock (Bazzill); gel pen (Marvy)

SIMPLE PHRASES

Goals for 2005 - *Becky Thackston, Hiram, Georgia*

Print goals on strips to communicate in an easy and concise way the things you want to achieve in the near future. This fun and lighthearted approach will allow you to fit several items on a page while not overpowering one element with another or ranking the importance of each. Goals to include can be related to career, education, family, hobbies, personal interests, travel or finance.

Every year Becky sets goals for herself. This year she put them in her scrapbook. She says she was "hoping this would help me complete them faster. By the end of February, I completed three." To quickly and concisely communicate her goals, she arranged the set of inked strips on the page.

Supplies: Patterned papers (Autumn Leaves, Mustard Moon); textured cardstock (Bazzill); die-cut letters (Sizzix); stamping ink; spiral paper clips; thread; pen

Create a list of random characteristics and special attributes that share the authentic, real you. Sit down, get in a spontaneous frame of mind and allow your mind to flood with the facts and details that make up your character. Include likes/dislikes, favorites, personal characteristics or any other obsession, confession or detail that gives readers the scoop on the one and only you.

When Mikki titled her page "Random Facts," she meant just that. She chose characteristics that describe her personality, her traits and her likes without giving deep thought to how they fit together. She also designed the page in a random fashion. After printing the words, she trimmed them into strips and added them to the page in an unplanned manner. Her color scheme brings a warm and earthy feeling to the page.

Supplies: Patterned papers (Scenic Route Paper Co.); specialty paper (NuArt Handmade Papers); textured cardstock (Bazzill)

REPETITION

Losing *- Julie Johnson, Seabrook, Texas*

Use repetition of key words to write a heartfelt poem. In this example, the depiction of what the subject is losing is compared to that of what she is gaining. By choosing one element to hinge each opening line of the poem, you can easily and creatively draft your journaling in a poetic voice.

Writing a poem can sometimes capture the emotion of a moment better than straight prose. Julie's sister, Jamie, wrote this poem to express her feelings for her daughter, Audrey. Julie included the poem as well as her own personal reflections of her niece and added it to her page. To create texture on her title, Julie stamped into dimensional paint that she spread onto the letters.

SUPPLIES: Patterned papers, decorative brads, pearl head pin, ribbon, and stickers (Making Memories); textured cardstocks (Bazzill); chipboard flower and letters (Everlasting Keepsakes); chalk inks (Clearsnap); fixative spray (Krylon); texture paste (Delta); flower stamps (Hero Arts); flower charm (source unknown); paper flowers (Prima)

Featuring a gesture of love, the American Sign Language version, Heather wrote about what the sign means to her family. It is a special signal they use whenever words are not possible. Heather's combination of stamping, hand-colored letters, vellum cut-outs and neutral papers brings out the youthful feel of the page.

Repeat a single key phrase to express the significance of those words when spoken in real life. Add additional explanatory journaling to share with readers the backstory and importance of those words.

SUPPLIES: Patterned papers (7 Gypsies); mini brads (ScrapArts); ribbons, vellum flowers (American Traditional Designs); photo corners (Heidi Swapp); hand stamp (Stampington & Co.); bracket stamp (Wendi Speciale Designs); label maker (Dymo); pen; cardstocks

REPETITION

Happy - *Doris Sander, Hermitage, Tennessee*

Journaling within frames is great for handwritten writing because it is in a contained space. The repetition of the boxes allows for repetition in the journaling as well.

Doris used this fun cardstock frame as a place to list the many ways the photo makes her happy. She combined the use of thick- and fine-line pens to enhance the sentiments. The vibrant colors and funky patterned papers coordinate with her son's pajamas and add to the young, playful theme.

Supplies: Patterned papers, pillow tag (Autumn Leaves); textured cardstock (Bazzill); cardstock frame (DieCuts with a View); letter stickers (Doodlebug Design); rub-on letters (Scrapworks); label holder (KI Memories); mini brads (Making Memories); pen

So Wonderful - *Sara McMartin, Dresden, Germany*

Begin each sentence of your journaling with a repeating phrase to emphasize the substance of the feeling or sentiment being expressed. In this example, the artist chose to journal along the border of the focal shape to keep the design balanced.

Following the outline of a specialized die-cut flower paper, Sara created a straightforward yet captivating page featuring her daughter. She echoed the die-cut shape by hand-printing her journaling around the petals and machine-stitching petals from the center of the flower.

SUPPLIES: Patterned paper, porcelain tag, epoxy letter stickers (Autumn Leaves); textured cardstock (Bazzill); ribbon (American Crafts); pen; thread

5 Steps - *Angelia Wigginton, Belmont, Mississippi*

If you're looking for a whimsical and lighthearted approach for documenting silly behaviors, hard-to-break habits or just downright unusual mannerisms, step-by-step journaling may do the trick. Break down each step in the same manner you would a recipe or set of instructions. Add a dash of humor for a truly tongue-in-cheek portrayal.

According to Angelia, getting her husband to actually sit in front of the camera requires some sweet-talking. When she finally achieved this goal, she created a comical page about the accomplishment. She wrote the text as if speaking directly to her husband, with each step featured on the page printed on cardstock, trimmed and highlighted by a small epoxy number.

SUPPLIES: Patterned papers (Basic Grey, My Mind's Eye, Scenic Route Paper Co.); epoxy letter stickers, rub-on fleurs-de-lis (Autumn Leaves); epoxy word (Provo Craft); chipboard frame, photo corners (Heidi Swapp); transparency tab (Creative Imaginations); number sticker (K & Company); rub-on letters and numbers (Making Memories, Scenic Route Paper Co.); photo turns (7 Gypsies); mini brads (Making Memories); stamping ink

A great way to structure step-by-step journaling is to sit down and think about what is going on inside the subject's mind as he or she performs the task. Then capture those thoughts on paper and embellish them with description and humor.

Greta says her daughter "seemed so methodical in how she was eating her ice-cream cone, that it was only natural that I use step-by-step journaling." For a whimsical page, she coordinated her patterned papers perfectly with her daughter's vibrant shirt.

Supplies: Patterned papers (My Mind's Eye); rub-on numbers (Making Memories); paper flowers (Prima); chipboard letters (Heidi Swapp); brads (Making Memories, Paper Studio); rub-on letters (Autumn Leaves, Provo Craft); ribbon (May Arts); photo corner (K & Company); acrylic paint

just the facts

Journaling on scrapbook pages is a way to document and reflect on the moments of your life. But with each fleeting moment, it sometimes becomes difficult to step back, observe the magic around us and record those precious details on paper. This chapter will show you ways to quickly and easily document the facts through interviews, calendars and lists. You'll be amazed to see that your words can be straightforward and to the point, yet still be penned with passion.

3

treasure (trezh'er) 1. accumulated wealth 2. something of great worth 3. irreplaceable; priceless

four

What is your favorite color? pink

What is your favorite animal? kitty cat

What is the first thing you want to look at in a store? toys

What is your favorite song? "Jesus Loves Me" and "If You Are Happy"

What is your favorite day of the week? Thursday

What is your favorite place to visit? Granna's, Aunt Cindy's, and the beach

What is your favorite thing to wear? a dress or a leotard and tutu

QUESTIONS & ANSWERS

Undivided Attention - *Courtney Walsh, Winnebago, Illinois*

Feature a kid's-eye view with a series of questions or statements punctuated with kid speak. The words children speak will probably come to you pretty easily, but if not, just tape-record or jot down their sweet chatter next time they engage you in conversation.

To highlight her daughter's inquisitive look peeking over the fence, Courtney listed a batch of questions representing "all the silly questions I get asked during the day," she says. Each quest for Mom's attention is written from her daughter's perspective. The design's muted tones bring out the warm highlights in the photo, and the handcut flower petals add a soft, feminine touch.

Supplies: Patterned papers, rivet (Chatterbox); rub-on letters (KI Memories); distress ink (Ranger); embroidery floss (DMC); pen; cardstock

Say What? - *Jennifer Hansen, Wellington, Utah*

Kids love to pepper grown-ups with all sorts of questions, leaving us bewildered and bemused at the their sense of wonder and amazement. Capture their imaginative queries on journaling strips. Layer and set them at different angles for added visual interest.

Jennifer pondered how to design a page for this photo of her son when he entered the room and asked one of his amusing questions. She realized that this inquisitive moment should be the focus of the page. Jennifer used it to capture several of his funny questions. By using earthy, distressed elements, she brought out the relaxed, humorous nature of the page.

SUPPLIES: Patterned papers (Creative Imaginations); textured cardstocks (Bazzill); brads, spiral clips (Creative Impressions); stamping ink; sandpaper

QUESTIONS & ANSWERS

Favorites at 3 - *Maria Burke, Steinbach, Manitoba, Canada*

Starting with just one question, record the delightful repartee between adult and child. Children can provide the greatest inspiration (and most humorous answers) to the simplest questions.

Talking with a 3-year-old can sometimes be a challenge, but mothers use their magic to draw the information gently from their little ones. Maria recorded the short conversation that finally came forth about Sarah's favorite things. For the design, she used colors that coordinated with Sarah's bright swimsuit, complementing them with warm background papers, bright white journaling strips and colored brads.

Supplies: Patterned papers (KI Memories, Li'l Davis Designs); monogram number (Urban Lily); letter stickers, index tab sticker (SEI); square brads (Making Memories); solvent ink (Tsukineko); ribbons (May Arts); cardstock

You don't have to be Barbara Walters to conduct a killer interview. Get the scoop by asking the questions that solicit the answers you feel are worthy of recording. These can be the simplest of queries, asking what every good reporter wants to know—how old are you, what are your favorites, what do you want to be when you grow up? Of course the list goes on, but you get the idea—nothing's off the record!

Dena interviewed her son to capture the thoughts and feelings of his life in fourth grade. After he answered the questions, she asked him to create the responses on a label maker. For a fun design, Dena inked the edges of her computer-printed questions and adhered them along with Ryan's labels.

Supplies: Patterned paper (Junkitz); chalk ink (Clearsnap); brads (Karen Foster Design); label maker (Dymo); wooden numbers (Li'l Davis Designs); fabric name patch (Weberley & Friends); embroidery floss (DMC); pen; cardstocks

QUESTIONS & ANSWERS

If You Had It to Do Again... - *Kristin Holly, Katy, Texas*

Use an interview to journal another person's insights or observations on any topic you feel worthy of exploration. In this example, the artist wanted to record her mother's thoughts on going to college and making serious life decisions for career and marriage. By using the interview as the journaling, it draws readers' attention and captures the voice of both the interviewer and interviewee.

Kristin wanted to know what, if anything, her mother would do differently in her life as a young woman. Her journaling block contains the prevailing thoughts of their conversations in a paraphrased version. Kristin used photos of her mother as a young woman and modified one in Photoshop to add a funky retro background.

Supplies: Patterned paper, oval tag (KI Memories); image-editing software (Adobe Photoshop 7.0); corner rounder (EK Success); vintage playing card; cardstock

Interviews are a great way to record the history of any relationship. They capture the precious details as well as the perspective of the interviewee.

Heidi asked her childhood friend various questions about their friendship so she could create a page about their many years together. She created a journaling block with one color representing each speaker. Letter beads show their initials at the beginning of each interchange. Heidi also strung the beads on wire in a circular pattern around a matted photo. A strip of tiny black-and-white photos lines the center of the page.

Supplies: Patterned papers (Flair Designs); textured cardstock (DieCuts with a View); letter stamps (Close To My Heart, PSX Design); craft foam, letter beads (Darice); colored beads (JewelCraft); fibers (Timeless Touches); ribbons (Michaels); wooden tag (Chatterbox); square punches (EK Success); twill (source unknown); rub-on letters (Scenic Route Paper Co.); square buttons (Making Memories); solvent ink (Tsukineko); wire; thread; acrylic paint

QUESTIONS & ANSWERS

Carly's World - *Tricia Rubens, Castle Rock, Colorado*

Use question-and-answer format to describe the feelings, desires or wishes of a child embracing another year. The same questions can be asked the following year, providing an annual documentation of a child's growth.

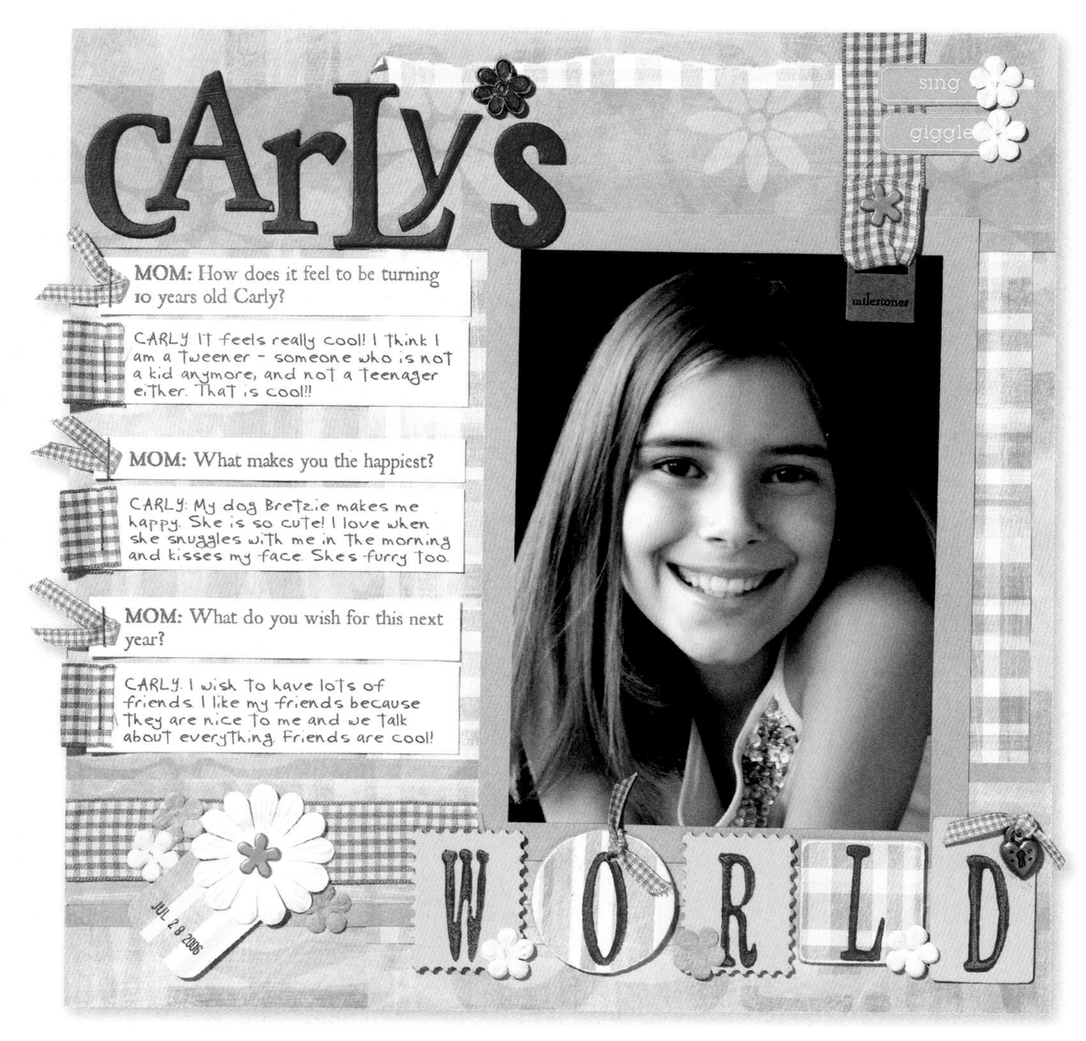

Tricia interviewed her daughter, Carly, about turning 10. To demonstrate the flow of the conversation, and to identify the speaker, she printed the journaling in two different font styles and colors. Each speaker is also represented by a ribbon of different widths. The bright and cheery colors reflect Carly's vibrant personality.

SUPPLIES: Patterned papers, chipboard shapes (Daisy D's); chipboard letters (Heidi Swapp); ribbons (May Arts, Michaels); flower and heart charms, flower brads, metal labels (Making Memories); paper flowers (Making Memories, Prima); foam letter stamps (Provo Craft); ribbon charm (K & Company); tag punch (Marvy); date stamp (Office Max); staples; acrylic paint; cardstocks

Just the facts, ma'am.
By using the who, what, when, where, why and how format, you can easily document the essentials of an event or experience. By separating each piece of information into a different block, you will create a visual hierarchy for your readers, allowing them to process the information easily. You will also allow extra room to expand on the important details.

In designing this page, Laurel wanted the journaling to be the focal point. Using the basic who, what, where questions, she gave the full account of the sweet surprise her daughters made. She designed each question using a different color. She says, "I chose the bright, multiple colors to reflect the warm memory of the cute and funny things my daughters do."

SUPPLIES: Patterned papers (Basic Grey); chipboard circles (Bazzill); paper flowers (Prima); face brads (Karen Foster Design); rub-on letters (EK Success); letter stickers (Déjà Views, Mrs. Grossman's); mini brads (Making Memories); chalk inks (Clearsnap); cardstock

8 Months - *Briana Fisher, Milford, Michigan*

Calendar-style journaling is a quick and easy way to record events or accomplishments. By creating a chronological timeline, you can visually enhance notes, lists or records that you may have in journals or notebooks. Ideas include baby's first year, courtship or engagement, pregnancy, school accomplishments, athletic or extracurricular activities throughout the season, and the first year of marriage. This style also makes it easy for readers to scan the information quickly.

With the help of a first-year calendar hanging in her son's room, Briana took quick notes each day of his accomplishments. When she created this page, she simply looked back at her notes to complete her journaling. She designed the page with the photos and journaling along the top and bottom of the page and added impact to the title by repeating the number "8" on a tag.

SUPPLIES: Patterned paper (Li'l Davis Designs); letter stamps, staples (Making Memories); tag (Rusty Pickle); ribbon (Close To My Heart); clock face (source unknown); brads; stamping ink; cardstocks

November - *Cherie Ward, Colorado Springs, Colorado*

For an interesting variation on a traditional timeline, you can employ circles or other shapes to give it a punch of visual appeal. For added fun, include an event such as an eclipse or a major news event to place the timeline in a historical context.

After several years of using a calendar to record the everyday events of her child's first two years, Cherie began to venture into creating other calendar formats. By using simple circular shapes, writing in colored pencil and featuring black-and-white photos, she created the perfect environment for a toddler's accomplishments. She chose sherbet colors to enhance the playful theme.

Supplies: Patterned papers (KI Memories); textured cardstocks (Bazzill); embroidery floss (DMC); distress ink (Ranger); circle cutter (Creative Memories); label holder, brads (K & Company); colored pencils (Sanford Corp.); ribbons (Lion Brand Yarn, Offray); staples

Andrew - *Holly Corbett, Central, South Carolina*

A fun technique to try for journaling is an acrostic-style list. Acrostic refers to the listing of words in which certain letters, most often the first, form a name or word. In this example, the artist chose to expand on her son's name by writing a short poem to express her appreciation for each moment she experiences with him. She repeated a key phrase at the end of five of the sentences to carry her theme of the joy of mother-and-son companionship.

Holly created an acrostic journaling block by using the letters in her son's name to begin each sentence. She wrote it like a poem, expressing sweet sentiments and meaningful thoughts about Andrew as her last baby. For a cohesive page, Holly featured green, blue and yellow, giving it a fresh, natural look that helped the photos pop off the page.

SUPPLIES: Metal letters (American Crafts); textured cardstock (Bazzill); paper flowers (Prima); die-cut squares and tag (QuicKutz); buttons, ribbons, letter stamps, triangular jump ring, date stamp (Making Memories); embroidery floss (DMC); photo corners (Pioneer); stamping ink

Bits & Baubles on Me - *Tina Werner, Otterville, Ontario, Canada*
Photo: Silver Parrot Studio, Simcoe, Ontario, Canada

Acostic-style lists can be used to share personal characteristics. Some items to include are astrological sign; color of eyes or hair; profession; favorite color, food, hobby or flower; a prized possession or anything else that spells out the true nature of the subject.

Tina employed acrostic-style journaling to list personal characteristics of who she is so that her children may one day know the younger "Tina Annette" and appreciate all the little things that made her unique. Floral patterned paper, silk flowers and a whispy font add a soft, feminine touch.

SUPPLIES: Patterned paper (Junkitz); stamps (Making Memories, Stampin' Up!); silk flowers, silver-rimmed circle tag, brads, fiber, transparency (from a monthly kit, www.thescrapbooksite.com); rub-on letters (Making Memories); crystal lacquer (Stampin' Up!); stamping ink; marker

LISTS

Some Things Change - *Elizabeth Cuzzacrea, Renton, Washington*

Then-and-now lists are a fresh and fun way to document the ways you have changed or grown over the years. Start by jotting down the items you want to compare—your hairstyle, what you do for fun, everyday tasks, etc. Then generate two lists comparing the ways in which you have changed, adding a bit of wit to each item.

Taking a look back over several years of dating, Elizabeth created this page to share the changes that have taken place in her relationship with Adam. Her first column notes activities they enjoyed when they began dating, and the second column contrasts what they do now. She finished the page with a message that their love has remained constant. To add some flair to the design, she used a mixture of stickers for her title and journaling treatments.

Supplies: Patterned papers (Basic Grey, SEI); round tag (Basic Grey); letter stickers (Basic Grey, Doodlebug Design, Making Memories); letter stamps (PSX Design); circle stamp (FontWerks); solvent ink (Tsukineko); chipboard heart (Making Memories); brad (American Crafts); thread

You can blend personal characteristics, favorites, special moments, accomplishments and milestones into one list that will serve as a record of an individual during a period of his or her life. Allow yourself to brainstorm all the things that he or she has said or done that has had an emotional impact. Ask yourself what things you want to keep close to heart, and document those on your pages.

"For me, journaling is the heart and soul of scrapbooking," says Jill, who has created a number of layouts like this one for her three children. Simply by listing meaningful things about various stages of her children's lives, she creates a living history of their growth. To bring this all-boy layout together, Jill converted her photo to sepia and used a range of blue and brown tones for the page.

Supplies: Patterned papers (Basic Grey); chipboard letter (Heidi Swapp); brads, hinge, label holder, printed twill, stencil letter, foam stencil letter stamp, diamond stamps (Making Memories); ribbons (American Crafts, Basic Grey); stick pin (K & Company); chalk ink (Clearsnap); acrylic paint; silk flowers; key

Who I Really Am Today - *Libby Jack, East Brady, Pennsylvania*

Create an all-about-me page with a bulleted list. Questions to spur ideas include: greatest hopes or fears, goals for the future, blessings, values or beliefs, precious memories, likes or dislikes, your opinion of the world, religion or politics.

Libby captured one moment in time by journaling her true and honest feelings. She took a look at her accomplishments, goals, surprises and fears and used bulleted lists to feature her reflections. Using a trio of colors—black, white and pink—she designed a feminine layout with torn and inked paper edges, stamped flourishes and pretty paper flowers.

SUPPLIES: Patterned papers, transparency border (Autumn Leaves); decorative foam stamp, metal letter charms, paper flowers, heart brads, chipboard letters (Making Memories); ribbons (Offray); epoxy stickers (Autumn Leaves, K & Company); solvent ink (Tsukineko); rub-on letters (Scrapworks); acrylic paint; brads; staples; transparency; cardstock

Go on a map quest. Use maps, diagrams or blueprints to point to places or locations of significance. This technique can create a timeline of events and can allow you to include a montage of different photos taken over a period of time.

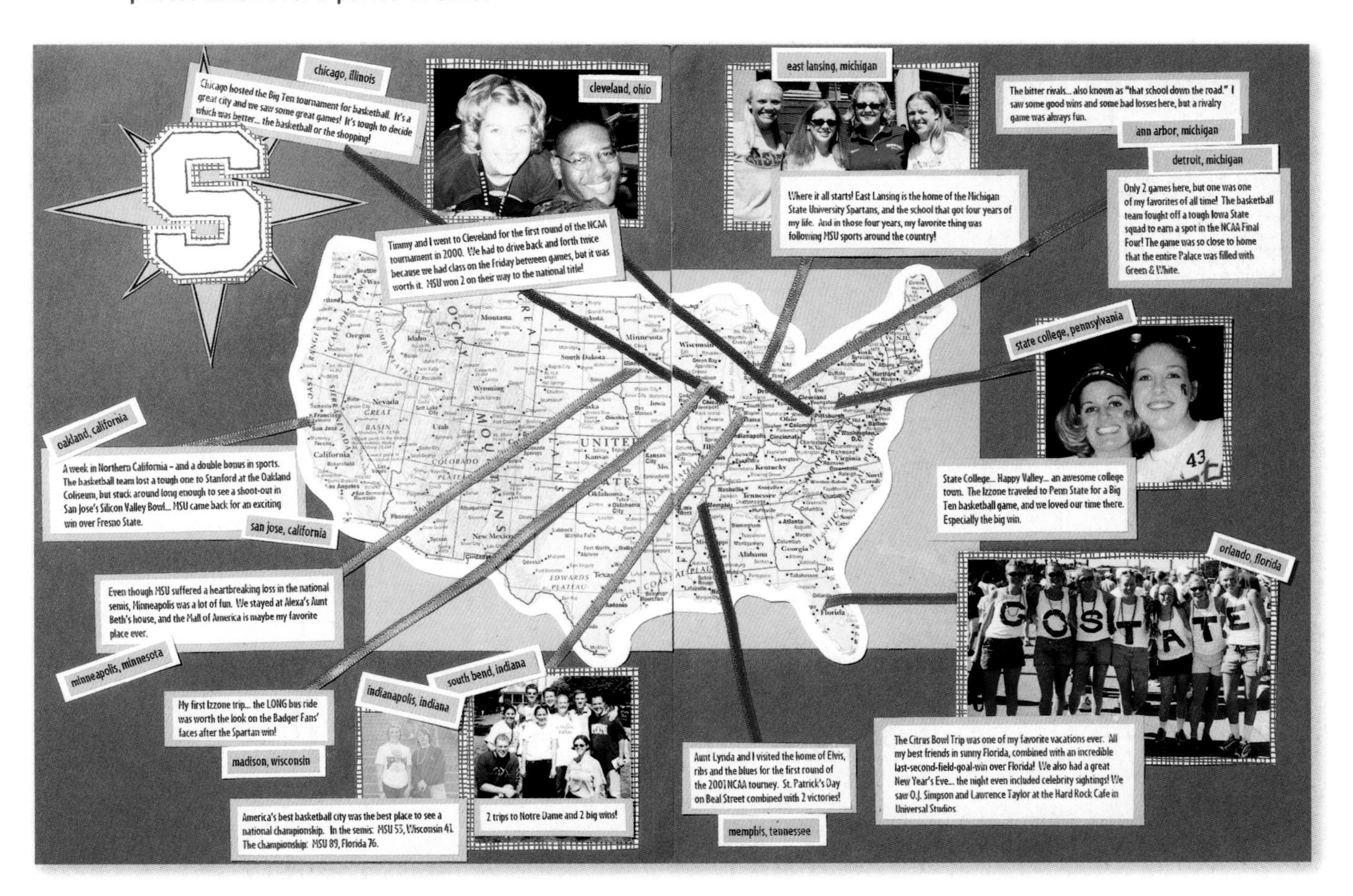

Did someone say road trip? Dana, a die-hard fan of the Michigan State University Spartans, documented the many trips she took to see the football and basketball teams in action. She showcased a map of the United States to highlight the great distances she traveled to see the teams. Green ribbons point to each city she visited, and journaling blocks give information about the city and her adventures there.

Supplies: Patterned paper (Paperbilities); ribbon (Offray); U.S. map (Rand McNally); cardstocks

This Is Me - *Nancy McCoy, Gulfport, Mississippi*

Create the perfect portrait of all your unique quirks and peculiarities by assembling a montage of qualities on a scrapbook page. Create your list first to determine the items you feel are most important and then arrange them on your page using a variety of colors and fonts to add visual interest.

As Nancy took photos of her shadow one day, she tried to make the camera disappear until she realized that the camera was such a part of her that she should celebrate it. She put the photos together with answers to a group of questions she was challenged with at a crop. Her digital layout features a bevy of fonts, one for each answer. She also printed in different colors to accent her neutral photos.

Supplies: Image-editing software (Microsoft Digital Image Pro)

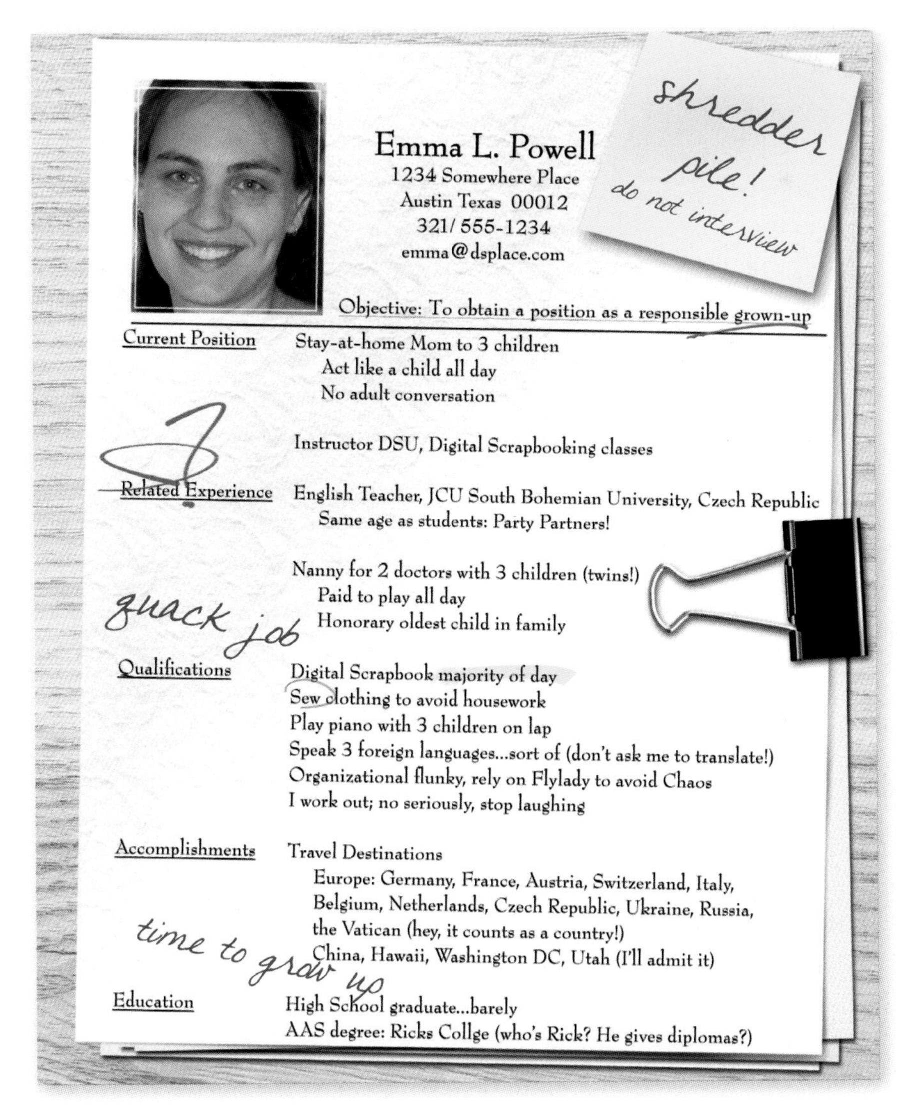

A résumé is a creative format for displaying personal attributes in a concise, organized and fun way. By adding a bit of humor, you can list the things about yourself (or another person) that make you who you are. Use standard headers such as "experience" and "qualifications," but respond with silly answers for a truly tongue-in-cheek portrayal of your "professional" life thus far.

Emma created a digital résumé for herself that spoofed her jobs as a stay-at-home mom and her former experience as a nanny. Each of the characteristics pokes fun at the many chores a caregiver has. Filling out her qualifications, she lists activities she enjoys, and her accomplishments highlight places she has traveled. To add wit to the page, Emma wrote notes that might have been written by a potential employer.

Supplies: Image-editing software (Adobe Photoshop Creative Suite); wood background, papers, clip (artist's own design)

The Good Stuff - *Dana Swords, Doswell, Virginia*

What's the good stuff according to you? Brainstorm the things in life you hold most dear and put them in list-format on your layout. Don't be afraid to invite loved ones in on the fun. Capturing the thoughts of another person may help you decide what's most important to you.

Dana created a page of what's important to her husband. First she asked him to write down his thoughts so she could make a list from his perspective. She opened the column with an introductory note and followed it with his quotes. Her delicate design features their newborn baby, Cole, a central focus of his journaling. Dana surrounded the photo with elegant floral patterned paper bordered by the more masculine striped paper.

SUPPLIES: Patterned papers (K & Company, Me & My Big Ideas); letter stickers (Crafty Secrets); ribbons (Offray); foam letter stamps (Making Memories); stamping ink; acrylic paint; thread; jewelry pin; cardstock

A Kind Heart - *Phillipa Campbell, Jerrabomberra, New South Wales, Australia*

Pay tribute to a loved one by blending precious memories with the things you love most about him or her. Rely upon your powers of observation and feelings to capture the person's true essence.

Using a treasured photo as the page anchor, Phillipa journaled some of her favorite qualities in her father. The first three journaling strips hold memories of his character and care of the family. The last strip shares a heartfelt thank-you. She used warm papers along with touches of nature to bring a comfortable and familiar feel to the page.

SUPPLIES: Patterned papers (Basic Grey, Chatterbox, K & Company, Scissor Sisters); stencil letter (Autumn leaves); metal letters (Making Memories); heart sticker, stick pin, epoxy letter sticker (K & Company); fleurs-de-lis stamp (Hero Arts); tags (EK Success); thread (DMC); photo corners (3L); ribbon (Me & My Big Ideas); twine; skeleton leaf; stamping ink; heart charm; jewelry tag; pen; cardstocks

get creative

Time to be courageous and exercise that writing muscle. Use letters, narratives, milestones, dialogue and other creative forms to write in an engaging and cohesive style that is all your own. Start by identifying the ideas or themes that you feel passionate about. Kristin Godsey, editor-in-chief of *Writer's Digest*, says "Just sit yourself down with a blank pad of paper and start writing. Once you get yourself going, it's easy to go back and pull out the ideas and sentences you like, edit them, and put them 'officially' in your scrapbook."

4

Senses
Sight
Just the vision of this photo brings back so many thoughts and memories about our quiet afternoon in the botanical gardens. The colors were so vibrant and bold, the contrasts so striking. Each turning of a corner brought new sights to behold - virtually a feast for the eyes.
Sound
I recall how peaceful and quiet the gardens were. There was a calming and rhythmic beat in the air. As we strolled through the beauty and wonder of the flora, I could hear the low and continuous hum of the creatures that live amongst the blooms. It was almost too serene to break with the sound of our own hushed voices.
Smell
Every blossom emitted it's own sweet fragrance, each one unique and distinct. I remember easily the way the smell of the garden enveloped me as I walked through the front gate. Words cannot possibly or adequately describe the aromatic sense provided by the combination of pleasant scents.
Touch
The texture of this hibiscus is detailed well in this photo and it evokes a memory of what it felt like as I touched the softness of its petals - so velvety and smooth. It had a delicacy that can't be matched by any man-made product, but only produced by wonders of Mother Nature herself.
Taste
What warm, sun-filled walk in the garden would be complete without the sweet taste of a cold ice cream cone? So smooth and creamy on the tongue, intensely rich and satisfying to the senses and always refreshing to the tired soul. It is an indulgent tradition we established on our first stroll in these elegant walkways.

LETTERS

Kindred Spirit - *Lisa Dixon, East Brunswick, New Jersey*

Letter writing is a great way to express thoughts and feelings while leaving a legacy for future generations. It's also a unique way to reflect or pay tribute to someone whose time on earth has expired but who is still alive in spirit. This format works particularly well for vintage layouts as letter writing was one of the few forms of communication available to our ancestors. Another option is to include an authentic letter from someone else expressing his or her unique viewpoints on friendship, life or love.

When Lisa received her great-grandmother's scrapbook, she knew she had a huge responsibility to take care of and preserve the contents. She wrote a letter to her great-grandmother, promising to take good care of it. To enhance this page, she scanned pages from the vintage scrapbook and cropped the images to fit on the page. Lisa used a few vintage touches such as buttons and hairpins for an authentic look.

SUPPLIES: Patterned papers (My Mind's Eye); chipboard shapes, textured cardstock (Bazzill); letter stamps (Hero Arts); chipboard letters (Li'l Davis Designs); deacidification spray (Krylon); rub-on letters (Making Memories); square tag (Anima Designs); coated linen thread (Scrapworks); vintage twill; button card; buttons; hair clips; rickrack; dress pattern; photo corners; vellum; stamping ink; pen

Signed, sealed, delivered—I'm yours. Letters featured on scrapbook pages need not be the kind that require postage. Love letters or love "e-mails" are perfect items to include as journaling as they document the "sweet nothings" expressed in the magical first days of falling in love. What better way to look back with fondness on flirty communication between you and your sweetheart.

From: Bootska Add to Address Book
Date: Tue, 12 Jun 2001 11:22:26 EDT
Subject: Rain Dance
To: emily

I'm glad we had our little chat last night, it clears up a lot of things and perhaps I won't be as apprehensive if something were to progress. I feel very comfortable around you, which in itself made me feel uncomfortable. You may not understand what I be's saying so I may explain it to sometime. You prayin for rain yet. I'll see what I can do on that end. Have a good day. TTYL

jmbs

Before Emily and Jay officially began dating, they sent flirty messages to each other via cyberspace. Like any girl in love, Emily saved the notes. She eventually printed her favorites and incorporated them into a page. To allow a number of her favorite messages to be read, she created a pocket over the bottom third of the page and tucked them inside.

Supplies: Patterned papers (KI Memories); letter stamps (PSX Design, Stampin' Up!); metal flower clip (Scrapworks); button (Doodlebug Design); stamping ink

LETTERS

Intelligence Vs. Beauty *- Courtney Walsh, Winnebago, Illinois*

Include words of wisdom in letter format to express the values and beliefs you hold most dear. In years to come, the individual you dedicate your letter to will cherish the insight you've passed on and engraved in their hearts.

Sophia,

You are so smart. Oh, I know, I must sound like a typical, bragging parent, but
the truth is, you really are amazingly intelligent. Before you were two, you knew
shapes, colors and the alphabet. You've just turned three and you can write all
the letters and are starting to read. I can't remember a time you didn't speak in
complete sentences. You can recite countless books and have a memory like a
steel trap! (I learned very early on I couldn't tell you we'd 'do something later'
because later would come and you would ask me to do it!) I've had grade
school teachers tell me how advanced you are—knowing what even first grad-
ers don't know. I really shouldn't be so surprised. Your daddy was 12 when he
started high school – yes, he was "promoted." And, I prayed you would be intelligent. That word always found its way into my prayers for you before you
were born.

But what I want you to know is that in this world, the value placed on beauty is
far greater than the value placed on intelligence. We grow up feeling we need
to be beautiful in every way. As girls, we feel the tremendous pressure to look
a certain way, to dress a certain way, to act a certain way... and most of those
"ways" don't involve intelligence. Now, don't get me wrong, I'm not saying you
shouldn't spend time on your appearance. Lord knows I'm a little too vain for
my own good, constantly thinking I need to do something to improve my imper-
fections. But if there's one thing I want to pass on to you, my sweet girl, it's
that your looks will only get you so far. Value that brain of yours. Love learning. Love wisdom. Love knowledge. Love knowing the answer to the question
before it is asked. And never, ever allow anyone to make you feel like it's not
"cool" to be smart. It is.

Remember, Sophia...
beauty fades... but wisdom lasts forever.

Love,
Mom

Courtney values intelligence, and in order to communicate that to her 3-year-old daughter, she wrote a personal letter talking about some of the challenging life issues she will experience as she grows up, encouraging her to value her own "smarts." Her page combines dainty flowered and striped papers with lovely black-and-white photos. She accented the spread with silver elements for just a touch of elegance.

Supplies: Patterned papers, stitched tags, stencil letter, rub-on letters (Chatterbox); metal letters, brads, heart clip, photo corners (Making Memories); label maker (Dymo); ribbon (Hobby Lobby); conchos (K & Company); paper clips; sandpaper; cardstock

From Tulum, Mexico - *Pamela James, Ventura, California*
Photo: Kelli Noto, Centennial, Colorado

Using a postcard is a simple and fun way to take your readers along on your journey through your favorite city or country. In addition, imagery—the use of vivid or figurative language to represent images—evokes mental images of a time or place and provides more than a play-by-play of an event or experience. "Turquoise ocean" and "lush green jungle" are good examples of imagery.

A real postcard provided the perfect place for Pamela to capture her recollections of a special day on her vacation. She addressed it, put a stamp on it, hand-printed her journaling and inked the edges for definition. To complement her design, she tucked the bottom corners behind her photos. The warm colors used on the page evoke the feelings of the sand, sea and sun of Mexico.

Supplies: Patterned papers (American Traditional Designs, K & Company); personal media cutter (Wishblade); word sticker (Destination Scrapbook Designs); cardstock stickers (K & Company); thread; pen; twine; stamping ink; cardstock

LETTERS

Be Yourself - *Doris Sander, Hermitage, Tennessee*

Add flair to a standard letter by printing or stamping larger letters over the whole. Not only will it add emphasis but will create visual appeal as well.

Doris printed her subtitle in monochromatic gray tones directly onto her page and added hand-printed journaling in black over the top. This subtly reinforced her hopes that her son will grow up to be his own person without following all the fads that surround him. She used gray plaid papers and contrasted them with colorful photos and chipboard title element.

SUPPLIES: Patterned papers (Basic Grey, Chatterbox); chipboard tag (Li'l Davis Designs); letter stamps (Li'l Davis Designs, Stampin' Up!); ribbon (Heidi Swapp); stamping ink; pen

Sometimes it's hard to get the words on paper—especially when the emotions involve fear or sorrow. But don't be afraid to write exactly what you feel. In fact, sometimes the best writing is generated when we are feeling the deepest of emotions. Adding this kind of feeling will add impact to your page and allow you to share your heart with those you love most.

From the first glance at this page, Suzy's 4-year-old daughter looks afraid. After reading the personal letter she wrote to her daughter, it becomes apparent that she is also struggling with the strong emotion. Since her daughter has a rare blood disorder, Suzy often faces fears about her condition. As she designed the page, she kept the journaling the central focus but added a tender matted photo and patterned papers to balance the design.

Supplies: Patterned papers (Scenic Route Paper Co.); chipboard letters (Making Memories); stamping ink; acrylic paint; pen; cardstocks

LETTERS

San Francisco - *Lora Covington, Superior, Colorado*

Use postcards to record your travel itineraries. You're likely to pick up postcards on vacation anyway, and your writing on them can serve as the perfect captions to your photos.

To help her remember all the wonderful aspects of each vacation day, Lora keeps a small file to hold memorabilia. At the end of the day, she takes notes about her adventures. When she is ready to make a page, she simply refers to the notes for that date. To bring together her page theme and design needs, she wrote her thoughts on the back of a postcard.

Supplies: Patterned paper, tag (Basic Grey); metal sun embellishment (K & Company); letter brads (Jo-Ann Stores); letter stickers (SEI); rub-ons (Creative Imaginations); postcard; pen

Incorporate memorabilia as part of your journaling to add flavor and visual interest. Choose a font that reflects the personality or tone of the layout.

Laurel gathered a few pages from her memory book at the end of her daughter Jordan's first year of kindergarten. She scanned several projects, adjusted the size and printed them to use on the page. Reflecting on the year, she wrote a letter to Jordan, complimenting her on the amazing growth that took place.

SUPPLIES: Patterned papers (Basic Grey, EK Success); border stickers (Bo-Bunny Press); ribbon (Offray); transparency; brads; cardstocks

LETTERS

Glee Mail - *Vanessa Spady, Virginia Beach, Virginia*

Keeping in touch across the miles can be difficult, but thanks to e-mail it becomes much easier. Include quotes or passages from e-mail correspondence that encapsulate your thoughts and feelings.

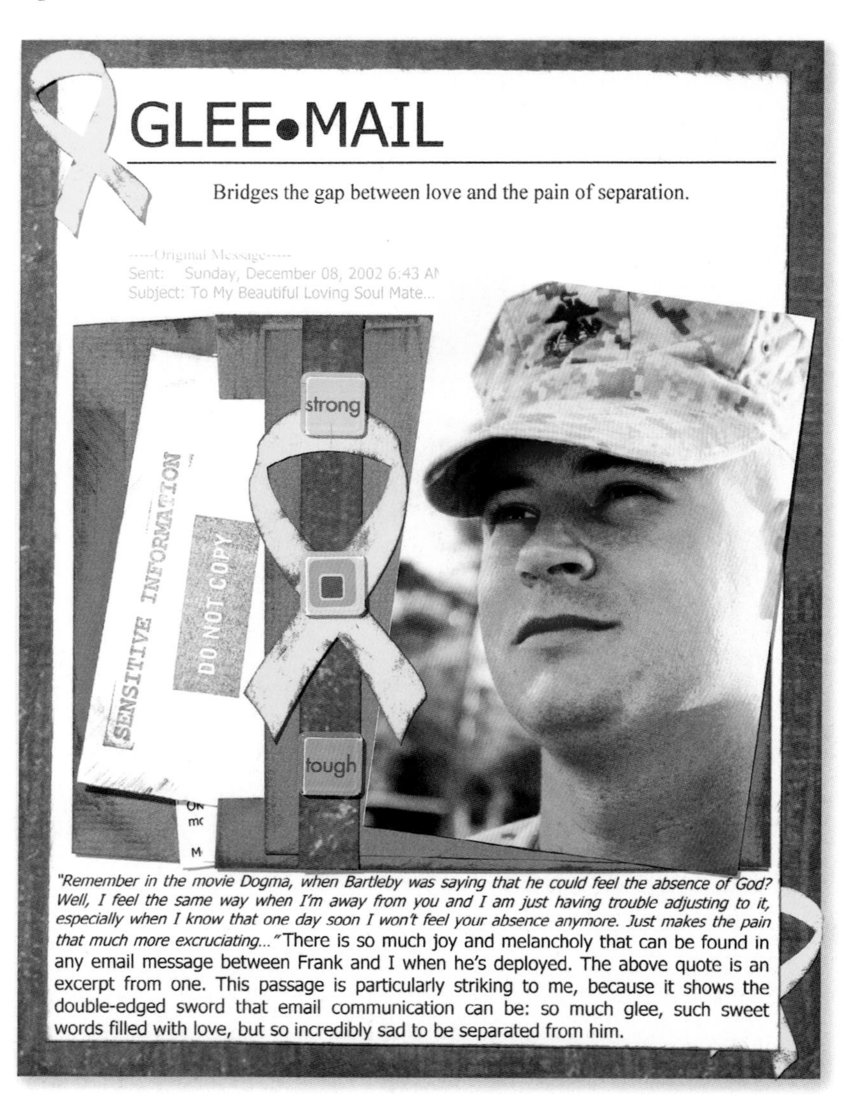

When a family member spends an extended time away from home, often the best way to communicate and stay connected is through the Internet. Vanessa chose an excerpt from one of her husband's e-mail letters to feature on the bottom of the page. She added her own feelings after the quote. A distressed envelope holds more personal messages that can be removed and read.

SUPPLIES: Patterned paper, die-cut ribbons (Memories In Uniform); envelope (Bazzill); word stamps (International Spy Museum); distress ink (Ranger); acrylic charms (KI Memories); cardstock

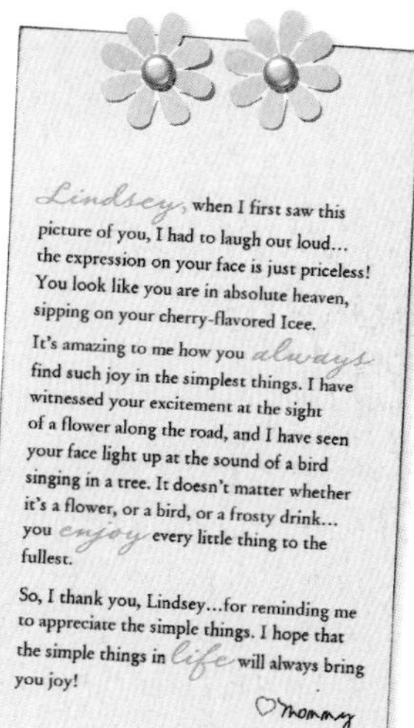

Lindsey, when I first saw this picture of you, I had to laugh out loud... the expression on your face is just priceless! You look like you are in absolute heaven, sipping on your cherry-flavored Icee.

It's amazing to me how you always find such joy in the simplest things. I have witnessed your excitement at the sight of a flower along the road, and I have seen your face light up at the sound of a bird singing in a tree. It doesn't matter whether it's a flower, or a bird, or a frosty drink... you enjoy every little thing to the fullest.

So, I thank you, Lindsey...for reminding me to appreciate the simple things. I hope that the simple things in life will always bring you joy!

♡mommy

Include a "secret message" within a letter to a loved one. This technique will require you to do a bit more planning. Draft your secret message first. Then write your supporting text to surround the message.

Hiding under Heather's focal photo is a journaling block with special meaning. She wrote the text as a letter to her daughter but highlighted special words. These red, cursive words add punch to the design but also give a heartfelt message within a message. Her title uses various sizes, shapes and textures to give the page a playful look.

SUPPLIES: Patterned papers (EK Success); ribbon (Offray); brads, letter brad stickers (Making Memories); frame charms (Provo Craft); fibers, key (Hot Off The Press); leafing pen (Krylon); letter stickers (American Crafts); rub-on letters (Autumn Leaves); solvent ink (Tsukineko); thread; cardstock; chipboard

NARRATIVES

Snuggle - *Sheila Doherty, Coeur d'Alene, Idaho*

Compose your journaling as a narrative—a story written with the first person point of view. If you choose to include the who, what, when, where, why and how into a single paragraph, you can share the important elements in a storytelling fashion, allowing the subjects of the journaling to shine.

Sheila's journaling about her two kids snuggling in the morning covers all the basic information of who, what, when, where, why and how. Using the six classic questions as a guide, she wrote the journaling in paragraph form, telling the story of that sweet morning. She used a combination of pinks and greens with subtle patterns to capture the moment and keep the genders balanced.

SUPPLIES: Patterned papers (Basic Grey, Déjà Views); ribbons (KI Memories, Michaels); metal charm (Pebbles); paper flowers (Prima); clear flower (Heidi Swapp); letter stamps (FontWerks); looped brads (Karen Foster Design); wooden letters (Li'l Davis Designs); acrylic button letter (Junkitz); embroidery floss (Making Memories); corner rounder (Carl); scalloped-edge template (Provo Craft); square brad (Creative Impressions); stamping ink; acrylic paint

Be an Original - *Kent Nichols, San Jose, California*

Use narrative format to tell the story of how you are unique and original. In this example, the artist chose to focus on one element—her name—to share how this aspect of herself makes her the person she is and how she has come to terms with other people's perceptions of it.

"I may be the only woman in existence with the name Kent," she says in her journaling. She recounts the story of how her mother liked the name and decided, girl or boy, that would be it. To allow the block of text to function as a design element, she printed it in a right-justified column onto her background. Kent's sepia-toned photo is enhanced by papers with graphic designs and muted colors.

Supplies: Patterned papers (SEI); metal phrase, heart eyelet (Making Memories); cardstocks

NARRATIVES

An Ironic Kind of Love - *Rebekah Bissell, Lakewood, Colorado*

A favorites page can focus on that one special item you hold near and dear to your heart. By telling the story of your love affair with your trusty iron, handmade quilt or Italian leather heels, you share with your readers an important piece of who you are and why that item adds value to your life.

Rebekah's relationship with her iron is a bit unorthodox in that it rarely touches her clothes. Her witty account is written from a crafter's perspective and shares a myriad of projects she uses it to create. To complement her theme, she used the iron to fuse together die-cut fabric shapes. Afterward, she zigzag-stitched the edges on her sewing machine.

Supplies: Patterned papers (DieCuts with a View); die-cut flower, tag and letters (Sizzix); fusible interfacing (C & T Publishing); heart brads (Target); square punch (Marvy); washers; fabric; shirt label; thread; transparency

Block journaling is an effective technique if you are going to include a large amount of text. This format will allow you to visually break apart the information so that it is easy to read. It also allows you to group the information into different categories depending upon your layout's theme.

When Barbara was faced with a challenge to do a page about someone she admires, she chose her husband. Many stories and thoughts flooded her mind. Using a block design allowed her to include a great deal of text. She used the outer edge for subheads and chose light and refreshing colors to lighten the mood of her deep sentiments.

SUPPLIES: Textured cardstocks (Bazzill); hole punch (McGill); rub-on letters (Making Memories); pen

For a Moment - *Lori Chissie, Hayden Lake, Idaho*

Express your feelings toward someone you love by writing a narrative in booklet form. In doing so you can celebrate the ending of an era and the start of new beginnings while letting that special person know how much he or she means to you.

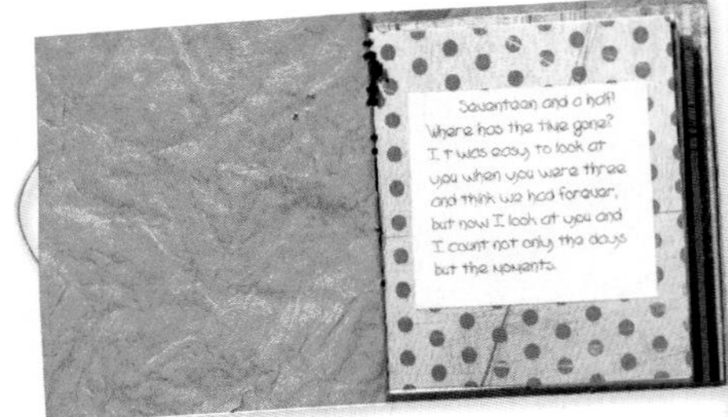

As Lori's son went into his senior year in high school with many new adventures in his life, she used lyrics from a song to express a bit of how she was feeling. She enclosed her own words that expressed her hopes and dreams for him in a small book attached to the spread. To symbolize the passage of time, she placed numbers along the bottom of the layout.

Supplies: Patterned papers (Basic Grey); textured cardstock (Bazzill); clock faces, leather paper, photo turn (Rusty Pickle); string closure (Colorbök); distressing kit, rub-on letters, mini brads (Making Memories); printed twill (Creative Impressions); photo corners (3M); embroidery floss

Capture the emotion and experience of precious milestones on scrapbook pages. Think of all the "firsts" in your life—the first day of school, first kiss, first job, etc. In this example, the artist chose to disclose her own feelings regarding her daughter going off to kindergarten in addition to details of the event itself.

Valerie's page features her daughter's big day leaving for kindergarten. She designed the page with bright, cheery colors and embellishments while her journaling recorded the challenge it was for her to let go and for her daughter to transition into the new environment. She designed the page around the journaling as it held the most important aspect of the page.

Supplies: Patterned papers (Foofala); buttons (7 Gypsies, Jesse James); chipboard monogram (Making Memories); photo corners (Heidi Swapp); paper flowers (Prima); ribbon (May Arts); embroidery floss (DMC); wooden tag (Chatterbox); rub-on words (Scenic Route Paper Co.); epoxy letter stickers, printed transparency (K & Company); vellum; cardstock

While You Were Sleeping - *Nic Howard, Pukekone, New Zealand*

Don't be afraid to journal about a devastating historical event. It records the event in history from the perspective of a bystander whose point of view will include the emotional impact a historical document might not.

Nic created this profound page that captures an instant felt around the world. While the focal photo shares a peaceful moment after a grand celebration, the journaling tells of the devastating earthquake and tsunami in Southeast Asia. These contrasting events, which happened at nearly the same moment, needed little embellishment to make an impact. Nic used a muted color palette of earth tones to keep the feeling subdued.

SUPPLIES: Patterned papers (Basic Grey); textured cardstocks (Bazzill); dimensional paint (Plaid); chipboard letters, rub-on words (Making Memories); walnut ink (Fiber Scraps); deacidification spray (Krylon); compass stamp (Oxford Rubber Stamps); distress ink (Ranger); acrylic paint; tags; date stamp; sandpaper; ribbon

Share unique physical attributes in narrative journaling. In this example, the artist focused on her son's smile and teeth to display her love for his quirky expressions. Brainstorm all the little things that you love about someone and highlight special words for added visual appeal.

Danielle printed her text in white on her sepia-toned photo. She highlighted special words by making them bold. To have space for journaling on a photo, she recommends being intentional when taking the photo and leaving space on either side of your subject. To create the curve design on the page, she covered the strips with a blue cardstock circular frame instead of trying to match every strip by trimming them individually.

SUPPLIES: Patterned papers (Basic Grey, DieCuts with a View); chipboard letters (Li'l Davis Designs); letter stickers (Basic Grey); corner rounder (Fiskars); pen; cardstocks

NARRATIVES

Theater Night - *Barb Hogan, Cincinnati, Ohio*

What activities bring you the most joy? Maybe it's strolling through the flower district in New York City on a warm summer afternoon, rock climbing in the Sierra Nevada mountains or leisurely enjoying your favorite magazine and cup of chamomile tea. We all have those guilty pleasures that infuse us with giddy delight so why not scrapbook them? To add even more fun, you can include memorabilia showcasing your favorite pastimes.

Beginning with the program from her favorite London play, Barb created a page highlighting her time living in the culture-rich city. Since the program's cover held lots of white space, she used the front of it to print much of her journaling. She added a black file folder to list her favorite plays. To lend an air of sophistication and mystique to the page, Barb designed it using primarily black-and-white elements.

Supplies: Patterned papers (Basic Grey, Cross My Heart); ribbons (May Arts, Michaels, Midori, Offray); chipboard letters (Li'l Davis Designs); file folder (Autumn Leaves); star brads (Magic Scraps); foam letter stamp (Wal-Mart); metal photo corner (Karen Foster Design); round gems (Westrim); washer word, star tag (Making Memories); pens; stamping ink; Rent program

Offer advice to future generations by recounting your own experiences and the lessons you gleaned from them. Not only will you offer bits of wisdom to others, but your own perspective and beliefs will be reflected in the time and place in which you lived. Think of the values or beliefs that are of utmost importance to you, and expand on how your own experiences led you to hold those convictions. An easy way to structure this is in numbered- or bulleted-list format.

College classes teach knowledge but, as Kent expresses in her journaling, life experiences sometimes teach us more. She created a list of five major lessons she learned while earning her degree. She shared various experiences that were unexpected turning points in her life. Her black-and-white photo is combined with purple and blue elements for a calm feel.

SUPPLIES: Patterned papers (Mustard Moon, Paper Loft, Scrapbook Wizard); brads (Making Memories); cardstock; ribbon; vellum

Tiny Glimpse - *Sherry Steveson, Wilmington, North Carolina*

You might not be able to see into the future, but your journaling can reveal all the wishes, hopes and dreams nearest to your heart. By formatting your journaling in a regular paragraph, you can allow your thoughts to flow freely.

The day Sherry got her new digital camera, she caught this image of her 9-year-old daughter. As she gazed at the mature image, she journaled how she felt she was seeing into the future. Leaving the text in paragraph form allowed the photo to take center stage. A printed advertisement inspired her design to which she added ribbons for pizazz.

Supplies: Patterned papers (Chatterbox, KI Memories); textured cardstock, chipboard circles (Bazzill); ribbon (May Arts); fibers (On The Surface); transparency; pin

Influence - *Carmel Flores, Westfield, Indiana*

Tell the story of a person who has shaped or influenced your life's decisions. How has that person's presence in your life made you the person you are today? Share the values or special traits of that individual and how they have impacted your life.

Inspired by a contest, Carmel created a page to honor the influence that her father has had on her life. She wrote a sizable journaling block explaining the many ways he impacted her. Carmel used a variety of fonts to showcase special words in her text. To embellish the page, she used both silk and patterned paper flowers, echoing the photo's fresh, outdoor feeling.

SUPPLIES: Patterned paper (KI Memories); textured cardstock (Bazzill); metal-rimmed tag, decorative brad, metal letter (Making Memories); letter sticker (Creative Imaginations); ribbon (Offray); silk flowers

NARRATIVES

The Complete Package - *Danielle Thompson, Tucker, Georgia*

Journal the story of how you came to fall in love with a hobby or passion. In this example, the artist explains in narrative form her love affair with fine art, photography and design, and how these elements combine to build the foundation for her as a scrapbook artist.

Danielle's narrative journaling creates a vivid picture of how her learning in college led her artistic loves to converge in the world of scrapbooking. In order to tell the whole story, she created a mini book with ledger tabs separating three of her passions. These hide a final block under the book summing up her feelings about scrapbooking.

SUPPLIES: Patterned papers (7 Gypsies, Anna Griffin, Magenta); beads (Blue Moon Beads); ledger tabs (Autumn Leaves); letter stamps (Hero Arts); rub-on word (Making Memories); ribbon (Michaels); rickrack (Wrights); trim (Hobby Lobby); decorative stamps (Outlines Rubber Stamp Co.); dimensional adhesive (JudiKins); silk flower; acrylic paint; stamping ink; transparency; cardstocks

Focus on the memories of home through narrative journaling. You can include the sensations a special place evokes, or you can put particular emphasis on the memories that were created within those walls. In this example, the artist chose to focus on the five senses to perfectly encapsulate the warmth and love that was felt within the walls she called home.

Read Christine's journaling and voyage to the old farm with her. See, hear, smell, taste and touch much of what she experienced when she and her family lived there. She paints a picture with her words that includes all the senses and the strong memories that she carried from there. Christine combined her photos in a continuous collage, giving the feeling of expanse that the property holds.

Supplies: Patterned papers (Scenic Route Paper Co.); letter stickers (Paper Loft, Scrapworks); chipboard letters (Li'l Davis Designs); mini brads (Making Memories); silk flowers

NARRATIVES

The Road to Indiana - *Gayle Hodgins, Philadelphia, Pennsylvania*

Can anyone say Holiday Road? Where does your car take you when you're in search of an adventure? By journaling voyages away from home whether it be hiking in Colorado, surfing in California or camping in the northern woods of Wisconsin, you can take your readers along on your exhilarating quest for excitement.

Gayle designed this page to tell the story of a long road trip. She printed the journaling on a transparency and placed it in a flip pocket that hangs over her photo. This placement not only creates an interesting visual effect but also covers "a not very good photo," she says. The journaling can be flipped up to reveal the photo or removed for easier reading.

Supplies: Patterned papers (Me & My Big Ideas, Mustard Moon); metal photo corners, flower stamp (Making Memories); mini bottle cap letters, stitching template (Li'l Davis Designs); ribbon sticker (Pebbles); pre-made state tag (Reminisce); brads (Carolee's Creations); round conchos, word inserts (Scrapworks); mini compass (Altered Book Club); flip pocket (C-Thru Ruler); twill (7 Gypsies); ribbon; acrylic paint; embroidery floss; transparency; cardstock

Share the legacy of a loved one by journaling a characteristic or trait they passed down to future generations. In this example, the artist chose to focus on one element—an open door—to symbolize how her mother embraced life with all its opportunities.

Deb's mother asked her to work some digital magic on a torn photo. She completed the transformation, and the photo took center stage for this page. Layering elements on the page gave Deb an interesting space to journal. She worked on her computer to get the right shape and then printed it onto faintly patterned paper. The fibers and old lace give the page a soft, feminine feel that reminds Deb of her mom.

Supplies: Patterned papers (Basic Grey, Scenic Route Paper Co.); ribbons (SEI); epoxy letter stickers (Karen Foster Design); letter buttons, gemstones (Magic Scraps); vellum envelope (EK Success); Rhonna Farrer's digital floral brush (www.twopeasinabucket.com); thread; lace; pen; transparency

PERSPECTIVES

Gracey's Diary - *Holle Wiktorek, Reunion, Colorado*

Writing from the perspective of a pet is sure to bring a smile to your face. Like humans, pets have their own unique personalities and quirks. Bringing that to life on a scrapbook page is a fun and easy way to include your pet in your memories.

As pet owners often do, Holle imagined what her dog might be thinking when they welcomed a baby to the family. She wrote the diary entries from Gracey's perspective, sharing how she must have felt with the tiny intruder in the house. Over time, the dog's behaviors changed, so Holle changed the tone of the entries. To show that it took time for Gracey to adjust, she dated each entry.

SUPPLIES: Patterned papers, tag (SEI); letter stamps, date stamp (La Pluma); mini brads (Creative Impressions); die-cut tabs (QuicKutz); distress ink (Ranger); ribbon (Offray); pen; cardstocks

Comfort - *Leah Zion, Indianapolis, Indiana*
Photo: Gregg Zion, Indianapolis, Indiana

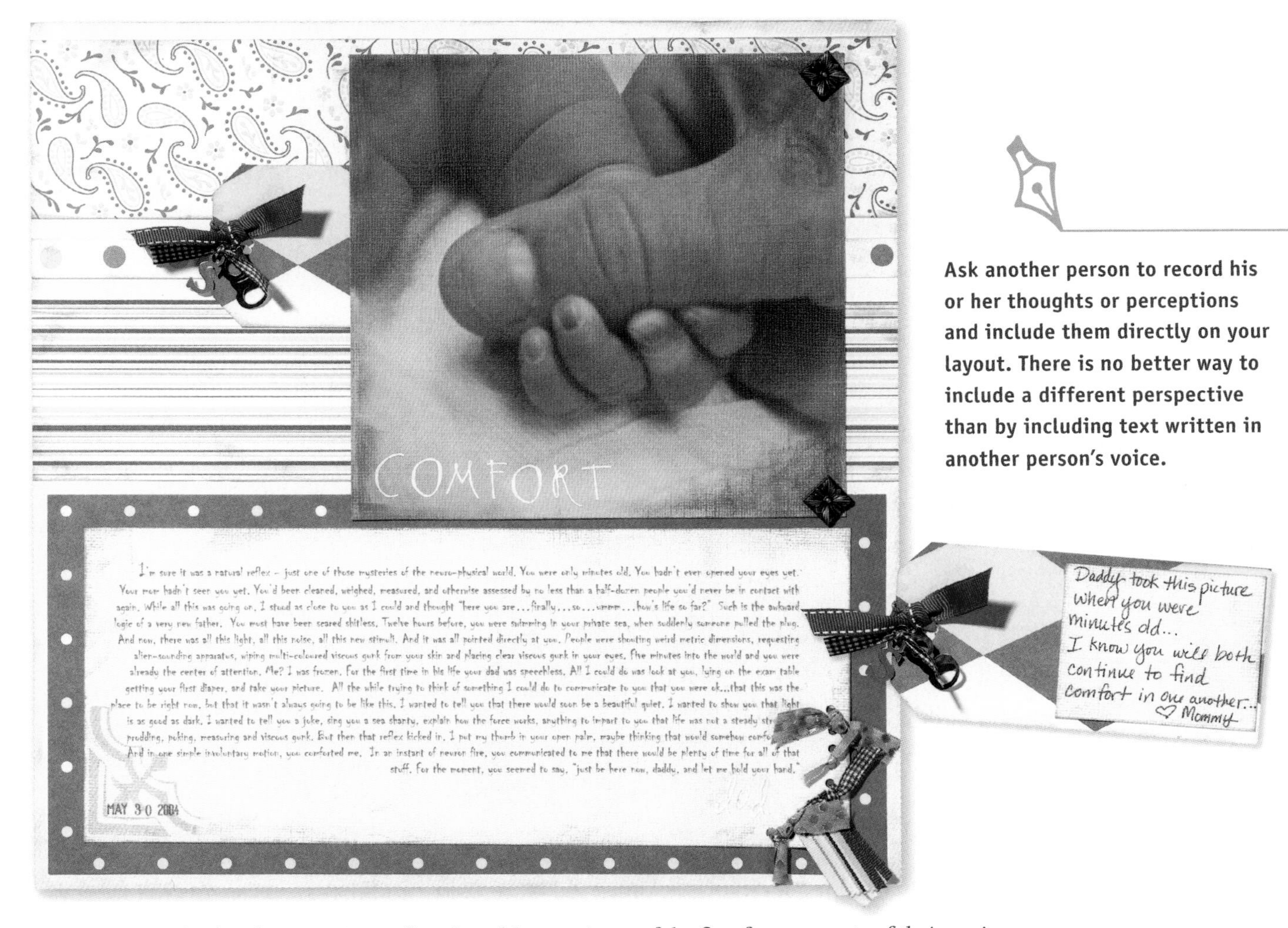

Ask another person to record his or her thoughts or perceptions and include them directly on your layout. There is no better way to include a different perspective than by including text written in another person's voice.

Leah asked her husband to write journaling from his experience of the first few moments of their son's life. The candid and poignant writing captures the moments that were witnessed only by Dad. Leah used the journaling as an anchor for the page. She featured a powerful photo of father and son holding hands minutes after birth. For a more delicate look, she converted the image to sepia and printed it on textured cardstock and added ink to give it the aged effects.

Supplies: Patterned papers, foam corner stamp, decorative brads, metal letters, rub-on letters (Making Memories); textured cardstock (Bazzill); distress ink (Ranger); ribbons (Michaels); date stamp

PERSPECTIVES

Pieces of Me - *Suzy Plantamura, Laguna Niguel, California*

Share goals or aspirations for the future or reflect on those from times past. List goals in paragraph form from the perspective of the subject. This format allows room to set up the backstory to tell why those goals are important and the chain of events that led to revisiting future plans and aspirations.

After waiting for her husband to write journaling for this page, Suzy wrote it for him. She asked for his approval and that is when he sat down and wrote it. She incorporated his words and theme into the design by cropping the enlarged photo into a mosaic to play upon the page title.

Supplies: Patterned papers (Basic Grey, Junkitz); chipboard letters (Heidi Swapp, Making Memories); chipboard circle (Li'l Davis Designs); epoxy letter stickers (Making Memories); ribbon (KI Memories); stamping ink; acrylic paint; brads; transparency; cardstock

Use a child's words to introduce a journaling block from his or her perspective. It will be a fun exercise to think of the ways he or she would react in a funny situation. To emphasize different perspectives, change the lettering to a different font.

Jennifer's son, James, told her quite plainly that he wanted to swim in the big pool. For the page, she recorded what he said and then created journaling that translated all the thoughts she imagined were going on in his mind. Using a color-blocked pattern that matched James' swim trunks, Jennifer jazzed up this all-boy page.

Supplies: Patterned papers (Daisy D's, Déjà Views, Karen Foster Design, Li'l Davis Designs); watermark ink (Tsukineko); wooden frames (Chatterbox); circle and word tags (KI Memories); eyelets (Karen Foster Design); brads (Colorbök, Junkitz); rub-on words (Déjà Views, Li'l Davis Designs); letter stamps (FontWerks); tab (Carolee's Creations); ribbons, tabs, metal label holder (Li'l Davis Designs); photo corner (Heidi Swapp); circle stamp (Hero Arts); acrylic paint; stamping ink; cardstock

TURNING POINTS & MILESTONES

The Classifieds - *Sharon Whitehead, Vernon, British Columbia, Canada*

Peruse the classifieds to find examples of words or phrases that you can bring into your own journaling. In this example, the artist used compare-and-contrast format to describe the ways in which she has changed, but in many ways, remained the same.

The highlight of Sharon's page is her Lost and Found journaling. She began by scanning a page from the local newspaper. She personalized elements on it by changing them on her computer. Sharon reinforced the look of a newspaper by keeping the columns justified and by using a font similar to what the newspaper used. She cut a red cardstock oval to resemble a circle scribbled on the column.

SUPPLIES: Image- and text-editing software (ArcSoft Photo Studio 2000, Broderbund Printmaster Gold 12); snaps, mini brads, photo turns (Making Memories); cardstocks

Use pictures in place of words to add visual interest to your layout. This technique, known as rebus-style journaling, is fun and easy and will add a lot of flavor to your design.

Intending to rekindle her appreciation for all she has, Courtney highlighted elements of her house she is most thankful for and took photos of them. She designed the page with the text as the focus, using the photos to represent words. This invites the reader into an interactive reading of the text. Her papers and embellishments, in blues and browns, coordinate with her home, inside and out.

SUPPLIES: Patterned paper (Mara-Mi); textured cardstock (Bazzill); text-editing software (Microsoft Picture It); ribbon (Michaels); chipboard letters (Heidi Swapp); distress ink (Ranger); rub-on letters (Chatterbox); acrylic paint; pen

2005 Goals - *Carolynn Jones, Medicine Hat, Alberta, Canada*

The design of a layout contributes to the way text is displayed. By printing text on tags and tucking them inside a hidden element, the visual pieces on the page remain front and center. Handwritten journaling flowing across the page adds a personal touch.

Like everyone else, I have hopes and dreams for the future. There are some days when I feel that is all I have - wishes, wants, etc. I wish I had more money, so I wouldn't have to count every penny and hunt for bargains. It would be nice to have a vacation every year - to show my daughter the world and let her experience the wonderful differences out there. I dream of owning my home instead of renting. I have a plan for this, fortunately, and I am determined to see this dream come true. My biggest dream, however, is nothing materialistic. I dream of seeing my daughter become a successful, self-confident and self-reliant woman. To do what she loves without hesitation. For her to become a Mom someday, and experience the joy that I do.

Setting goals is not new to Carolynn, but scrapbooking is. She took up the craft about a year and a half ago. Motivated by a challenge to create a page of goals, she had so much to say that she created two mini books. Carolynn tucked the mini tag book behind the soda-can-inspired swoosh pocket, and she adhered the accordion book to the bottom of the page and held it closed with a photo turn. Before putting together this multi-layered design, she sketched it on paper.

SUPPLIES: Patterned papers (7 Gypsies, Basic Grey); foam letter stamps, brad, photo turn (Making Memories); letter stickers (Basic Grey, Sandylion); fibers, time stickers (Sandylion); acrylic paint; stamping ink; pen; chipboard; ball chain; tags

Use then-and-now journaling to capture different stages of life. Incorporate short phrases or sentences to show the unique comparison and convey how the individual has changed over time.

Allison. 2 years old. A little girl. So cute and eager to learn. When you were born and they first placed you in my arms I looked at you and begged you not to ever grow up. You seemed to comply, for a while anyway. You needed me a lot. I helped you get dressed, you wanted to be carried everywhere, I'd do your hair everyday. I took you everywhere. I was the center of your universe. My little girl with cute round cheeks and curly hair.

Laura wants to slow down her daughter's growing up as many moms do. To preserve that thought, she created this page comparing her daughter at 2 years old and now at 7. Placed under the photos, her words echo from one block to the next as she repeated similar themes but updated the information. To highlight her title, Laura stamped letters on colorful patterned paper while the rest of her page remained black and white.

Supplies: Patterned papers (Carolee's Creations, KI Memories); die-cut clocks (KI Memories); ribbons (May Arts, Offray); gaffer tape (7 Gypsies); foam letter stamps (Making Memories); rub-on letters (Creative Imaginations); brads; acrylic paint; paper clips; stamping ink; cardstock

Defining My Life - *Amber Baley, Waupun, Wisconsin*

Describe an important life-changing moment by including your emotional reactions to startling news. It's likely your readers will be able to identify with your surprise or fear that accompanied such a moment, and they'll know a little bit about how your experience impacted your life today.

DEFINING MY... LIFE

I had the world in my hand. I was on the brink of eighteen. I had high school graduation pending, with a college scholarship at a school away from the small town that I had grown to hate. My parents even gave me a taste of the freedom I so longed for, by leaving me home alone while they visited my grandparents in Florida for two whole weeks. I looked forward to my senior class trip we would be embarking on the very next day. You can imagine my excitement.

In the midst of all my anticipation, I harbored a tremendous fear.

I had read the instructions several times over the night before, and had concluded that it would be best if I did it in the morning. I snuggled into my parents queen size bed, and found comfort in my mother's favorite quilt. I tossed and turned in the covers, uncomfortable from a full bladder I had purposely failed to empty and the knowledge that, come morning, I would have an answer. Finally, at three a.m., I tiptoed upstairs to my bathroom, clutching the Walmart bag in my hand as I went. I had driven 30 minutes away to pick up the pregnancy test, so that no one would discover my secret. I read through the instructions one final time and performed the test with the utmost precision. I knew I would have to wait three minutes for a result, but I couldn't take my eyes off the little test square. I watched as the liquid approached the window. In a matter of seconds, a pink plus sign appeared. It took less than a minute for my life to take a turn in a different direction. This moment defined who I was, and who I would become.

While my classmates screamed wildly and raised their hands in the air on the roller coaster at the Mall of America, I stood on the sidelines and watched, feigning a headache. When my classmates ordered coke and other caffeinated drinks, I ordered 7up. When my classmates soaked in the hot tub, and rested in the sauna at the hotel, I stayed in the pool. The morning I returned home from my class trip, I made a call to the doctor. I set up an appointment for one week later. Immediately afterward, I lost my breakfast to the toilet bowl. This became a morning ritual, that continued into the afternoon and evening. When the doctor confirmed my results, I made a follow up appointment for a month later, and instructed the receptionist not to bill my insurance company. I paid cash for the visit. I carried my secret with me for three months. In that time, I told my parents that I had decided to take a year off before I pursued college. You can imagine their disappointment in me. But I knew that disappointment would pale in comparison to what they would feel when I shared with them the truth.

I will admit that I did not make all the right choices. But I am proud that I put the infant growing inside me at the center of all those decisions. I tried to do what was best for him, and for us.

When I look at this picture, I must say goodbye to the girl I could have been. Instead, this experience defined the woman I became.

Amber wrote candidly about a moment that changed her life. Just before departing on her high-school senior trip, she discovered she was pregnant. She captured the feelings she had about watching the fun her friends had while she took care of the baby inside her. By creating a matchbooklike cover, she hid the journaling under a flap at the bottom of the page.

SUPPLIES: Patterned papers (Basic Grey, Chatterbox); rub-on letters (Autumn Leaves); embroidery floss (DMC); distress ink (Ranger); thread; silk flower; button; cardstock

Losing My Baby - *Denise Tucker, Versailles, Indiana*

Allow your journaling to focus on how an important event marks a turning point in a child's life. Examples can include taking first steps, losing a tooth or learning to read.

Mothers of any generation can relate to the bittersweet feeling towards a child's losing a tooth. Denise's journaling celebrates the occasion and gives a place for her to share her feelings about a few monumental changes in six years. Denise's focal photo captures the moment and her journaling immortalizes it.

Supplies: Patterned papers (Basic Grey, Karen Foster Design, Rusty Pickle); wooden letters (Wal-Mart); metal letter tiles, rub-on letters, mini brads (Making Memories); ribbons (American Crafts, Offray); chipboard (Rusty Pickle); distress ink (Ranger); acrylic paints; stamping ink; antique buttons; envelope template; cardstocks

The End - *Colleen Stearns, Natrona Heights, Pennsylvania*
Photo: Thomas Culleiton, Natrona Heights, Pennsylvania

By journaling difficult moments, you can use scrapbooking as a means to look forward and embrace the adventurous path ahead. It may force you to deal with emotions from the past, but you can get down on paper the ways in which you've grown and how the experiences you've had have made you the person you are today.

Sometimes a peek into a memorabilia box sparks thoughts and emotions that become a page. Colleen decided it was time to put her challenging high-school days behind her, and she designed the page to bring closure. She scanned her graduation memorabilia and included the images in her design. Colleen wrote her journaling recounting the feelings and attitudes she experienced. The muted browns help convey the mood of those years.

Supplies: Patterned papers (Scenic Route Paper Co.); letter cut-outs (Foofala); dominoes (Boxer Scrapbook Productions); distress ink (Ranger); walnut ink (Rusty Pickle); ribbon (Jo-Ann Stores); cardboard; graduation memorabilia; lace; cardstocks

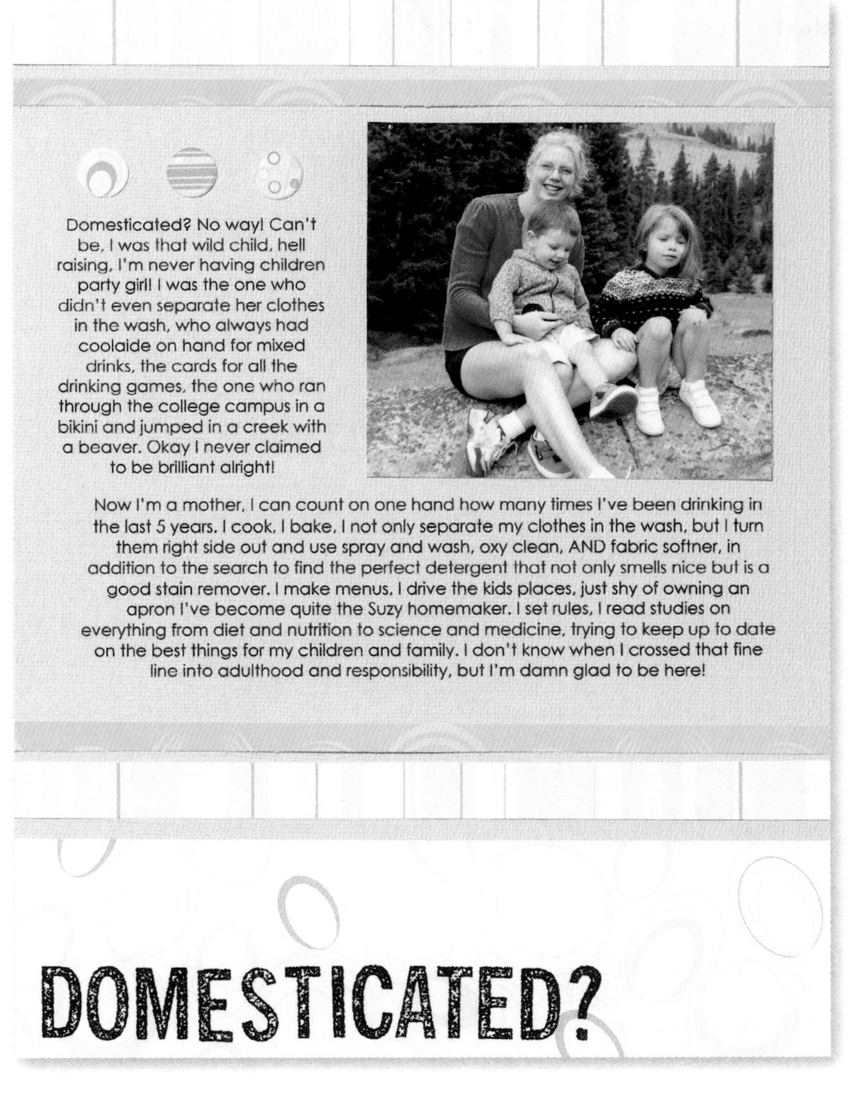

Do you feel that the hands of time have changed your perspective or outlook on life? Turning-point journaling is expressing the ways in which your lifestyle or attitude has changed as a result of the path you have chosen. Readers will appreciate seeing your new frame of mind and how it has shaped you as a person. They may even glean some of your wisdom and apply it to their own lives.

An e-mail message from a friend got Courtney thinking about how much she had changed since her carefree college days. Courtney created this page to show some of the specific ways that being a mom has changed her life. She wrote the journaling in two blocks, featuring the contrasts from then and now. She gave her page a retro feel by using hip papers with graphic images and coordinating epoxy stickers.

Supplies: Patterned papers, epoxy circle stickers (Autumn Leaves); rub-on letters (Making Memories); cardstock

Living It Right - *Renee Coffey, Lilburn, Georgia*

It's easy to record how far you've come whether it be in marriage, career or a hobby you pursue with passion. Write your accomplishments and milestones in sentence form and, for added fun, use them to border your page.

Renee surrounded her photo block with hand-printed journaling that gave a framing effect to it. By adding meandering lines of machine-stitching inside the frame lines, she gave it a carved look. Around the outer edge, Renee printed various memories from many years together. Adhering black-and-white images beside color ones gave more punch to her photo block.

Supplies: Patterned paper, pillow button, epoxy stickers, rub-on flowers (Autumn Leaves); letter stickers (Li'l Davis Designs); ribbon (Offray); pen; thread; cardstock

Every accomplishment is worth recording. Engrave the moment in time by capturing the true essence of each milestone in journaling. In years to come, you'll look back with fond remembrance.

Amy, proud aunt of Jacob, captured this monumental time of growth. She shared some of the basic physical milestones he achieved and some of his baby babblings. She made a few words bold and italic to give them special importance. For a fun kick, Amy kept her colors muted except for the punches of orange cardstock.

SUPPLIES: Patterned papers, stencil letter, ribbon, rivets (Chatterbox); vellum; corner rounder; cardstocks

FAIRY TALES

The Lady - *Sharon Laakkonen, Superior, Wisconsin*

By writing in fairy tale voice—using words or phrases that mirror the classic language found in well-known and beloved fairy tales—you can record a real experience or write a fictional tale of your own.

Sharon's daughter Brittany grew up with a flair for the dramatic and a love of fairy tales. When she participated in a neighborhood production of The Lady of Shalott, Sharon wrote the journaling as a fairy tale opening and closing the story with "Once upon a time" and "happily ever after." She framed the large photo with patterned-paper blocks, punched flowers and meandering machine-stitching.

Supplies: Patterned papers (Imagination Project); flower punch (Emagination Crafts); square brads (Queen & Co.); ribbons (May Arts); acrylic letters (Go West Studios); solvent ink (Tsukineko); diamond and circle stamps (FontWerks); distress ink (Ranger); paper flowers (Doodlebug Design); acrylic paint; thread; cardstocks

Happily Ever After - *Vicki Boutin, Burlington, Ontario, Canada*
Photo: Sheila Smith, St. Catharines, Ontario, Canada

Document your hopes and dreams or the journey of a lifetime by writing in this enchanting style. Peruse folk tales, myths, legends, fables, epic poems and nursery rhymes to find examples of language and usage.

Vicki says, "When I was a little girl, I had quite an active imagination and big dreams!" Her journaling highlights a few of those dreams from different vantage points in her life. Each block's text mirrors the next to keep them cohesive while the simple design allows the photos and title to shine.

Supplies: Patterned papers (Scenic Route Paper Co.); rub-on letters (Making Memories, Me & My Big Ideas); leather label holder, brads (Making Memories); photo turns, jeweled flowers (source unknown); thread; stamping ink; pens; cardstock

SCRIPTS & DIALOGUES

My Story, My Words - *Courtney Walsh, Winnebago, Illinois*

Add cinematic sizzle to your dialogue by formatting it like a traditional Hollywood script. This doesn't require storyboards or set design—just a whole lot of creativity and a flair for the dramatic.

The stage is dark. On it sits one woman, Courtney. She is preparing to perform her original play, a surprise hit with audiences and critics alike. She is dressed in black and sits on a stool CS.

Lights up.

Courtney: I had a dream the other night. It was years into the future and I was no longer alive. I could see my family, my great- great grandchildren. *(lights up SR where we see a mother and her two children, they are seated on a couch, reading a story.)* They were beautiful. And instantly, I was struck with this unexplainable fear. Fear of being forgotten.

(She stands, walks down center)

Oh come on, we all think this way, don't we? We all want to leave our mark. Make a difference. Be remembered.

I used to want to be famous. An actress – go figure. I thought if I were famous, I would somehow be immortal. Everyone would remember me. But now that I'm a little older, a little wiser, I realize that's not really true.

The family SR comes to life.

Great Grandson: Mommy, who's that lady? *(he is pointed to a photograph on the table)*

Mom: Oh, honey, that's your great-great grandmother. *(pause)* Her name.... was Courtney.

Great Grandson: Courtney? That's a funny name.

Lights fade out on the family.

Courtney: Someday, I'll be a photograph on someone's wall, in someone's photo album. I'll just be another old lady with a funny name. Someday my story won't be told anymore... unless I tell it to someone now.

That's why you're here. To hear my story. And everyone has a story. Mine is still being written, but rather than allowing people who don't really know me to put the pieces of my puzzle together, I'm going to make it easy for them. I'm going to tell it. In my own words. With my own inflection. And odds are, someday, when my great-great grandchildren are looking through a scrapbook of my life... they're going to hear my voice echoing through the pages.

Since Courtney loves to write plays and skits, translating the medium into her scrapbook journaling came naturally to her. Included in the mini book script are stage directions, lighting cues and of course, dialogue. Any reader of the mini manuscript can imagine the scenes as they might be played out. To highlight some of her favorite quotes of the play, Courtney wrote them on tags and tucked them into pockets she created using patterned-paper strips.

SUPPLIES: Patterned paper, tags (Chatterbox); ribbons (Making Memories, M&J Trimming, Offray); photo corners (Pioneer); brads (Making Memories); watercolor ink (Tsukineko); office clips; pen; corner rounder

When your child learns a new word, you expect to hear it a LOT.. well..one fateful night you learned a new word that would become a huge part of my memory of that evening.

Nate came home from work one evening with long stem white tulips for me. It was such a lovely surprise especially because tulips are my favorite. After dinner he went back into your room to talk to you and I was not allowed back there to hear what was going on.

You came running out about 15 minutes later and pulled me aside.

"Mom..*HYPOTHETICALLY* would you say that the beach is a romantic place to be proposed to at?"

"Umm..sure"

You ran backinto the kitchen to talk to Nate. Came back 5 minutes later.

"Mom..*HYPOTHETICALLY* if you were *HYPOTHICALLY* proposed to at the beach would you think that was *HYPOTHETICALLY* romantic.. *HYPOTHETICALLY* of course"

WHAT???

Of course Nate did propose that evening at the beach.

He had asked your permission for my hand in marriage and had used the word "hypothetically" to ask about possible proposal sights. He had no idea that you came out to ask me these questions. We found such humor in your use of the word. You thought you were being so sneaky..

Sometimes you are so darn cute Alex!!!

Kids say the darnedest things. Remember how much fun it was to learn new words and use them in conversation? Document the moment a child took in new words in dialogue format. You're sure to get a giggle from his or her creative use of language.

Just a few short months after her husband proposed, Jennifer scripted the foretelling conversation that took place between her and her daughter. She wanted to remember the encounter just as it happened and a dialogue account preserved the interaction. Her design features subtle colors and a captivating black-and-white photo of her daughter.

Supplies: Patterned papers (KI Memories); textured cardstock (Bazzill); metal eyelet letter, foam letter stamps, rub-on phrase (Making Memories); circle punch (Marvy); corner rounder (EK Success); epoxy letter stickers (source unknown); stamping ink

SCRIPTS & DIALOGUES

Food Network Canada - *Nicole Cholet, Beaconsfield, Quebec, Canada*

Perhaps you have just one important goal you want to document. By using dialogue, you can express that aspiration (or that of someone else) while adding humor and wit as well.

Coming soon to
Food Network Canada...
Calories
With renowned pastry chef
Samuel Goldwax

"Mom, have you ever been on Food Network Canada?"

"Umm...No. I haven't. Why do you ask"

"Because I'm going to be on Food Network Canada some day!"

"Oh yeah? Are you going to be the next Bobby Flay or will you take over on Sugar?"

"I think I'll be on Sugar, like Anna Olson. I'm going to create cool desserts and then show everyone how to make them. I've already started getting ideas."

"Sam, that's pretty cool! Are you going to go to cooking school when you get older?"

"Of course! But mom...Can I help make dinner tonight?"

" Sure thing, little man!"

"So, what are we making?"

JUNE 2005

In a short conversation with her son, Nicole discovered he had high-reaching goals in the culinary arts. She jotted down the conversation and took a photo to represent the day when he might achieve his goal. The page resembles a television advertisement for a cable food network with its clean, graphic look. Whether he stays on this career track or moves on to another, Nicole has recorded his passion at a young age.

SUPPLIES: Textured cardstocks (Bazzill); snaps (Doodlebug Design); letter stickers (Doodlebug Design, Provo Craft); ribbon (Making Memories)

Capture a spontaneous moment by including action words within a dialogue. This will add a little bit of flavor to a humorous recount of an impromptu moment.

Tracy combined her lively photo with anecdotal journaling that recounts the story of a summer-day dousing. Her text mirrors the conversation that unfolded. By including the actions in parentheses, Tracy gave a more complete picture of how the wet event transpired. She kept her design simple to give the attention to the photo and journaling.

SUPPLIES: Textured cardstocks (Bazzill); word sticker (Bo-Bunny Press); sun charm (source unknown)

PHOTOTELLING

When I Watch My Children - *Vicki Boutin, Burlington, Ontario, Canada*

By using your journaling as your primary design element, you can keep your layout clutter-free and focused on the important message you are trying to convey. Rebus journaling—using photos in place of words—is a fun technique that adds flavor and spice to your artwork.

Vicki says, "By using photographs of my kids and me and incorporating them directly into the journaling, this page takes on a life of its own." To design the page, she began by journaling, keeping in mind the photos she had available to use instead of words. Vicki laid her photos on the page and added the journaling around them, and used a white gel pen to add charming doodles around various page elements.

SUPPLIES: Patterned paper (Imagination Project); paper flowers (Prima); mini brads (Making Memories); chipboard shapes (Bazzill, Heidi Swapp); rub-on images (Imagination Project, Making Memories, Me & My Big Ideas); letter stamps (Scraptivity); pen; thread; cardstock

Lost - *Danielle Thompson, Tucker, Georgia*

Danielle journaled about the feelings of loss she experienced after Hurricane Katrina. She began by featuring a photograph she took at a New Orleans cemetery just two months prior to the devastation. In image-editing software, she used a text-wrap feature to allow the words to wrap around the image and highlighted words that most accurately communicated her deep emotions.

SUPPLIES: Patterned papers (American Crafts, Scenic Route Paper Co.); acrylic letters (American Crafts); foam letter stamps (Li'l Davis Designs, Making Memories); watermark ink (Tsukineko); definitions tape (7 Gypsies); acrylic frames (KI Memories); pens; foam; cardstock

Wrap text around a photo for astonishing visual impact. Whether you hand-write your journaling or print it directly onto the photo, it is sure to make your words pop.

WORD PLAY

The Art of Relaxation - *Andrea Lyn Vetten-Marley, Aurora, Colorado*

Erasure journaling is an altered-book technique where a piece of literature (book, magazine article, newspaper, pamphlet, etc.) is modified to highlight key words within a block of existing text. This technique is a bit more challenging as it requires planning and searching within text for the perfect message. Peruse a variety of sources and take time scanning the words to find the message you want to say.

Andrea enjoys working with vintage magazine articles to create journaling blocks. By making two photo-copies of the original article, she can use one to map out her journaling and the other to create the block. She began by "painting" masking fluid over the words she wanted to protect. After allowing the fluid to set, she applied quick-drying alcohol inks to the rest of the block in a calico pattern. Andrea then removed the masking fluid to reveal the words that make up the journaling and added stamped words to fill in missing words.

Supplies: Magazine articles (Delineator, 1875; Etude, 1909); alcohol inks (Ranger); letter and number stamps (Making Memories); beads (Westrim); masking fluid; vintage rickrack; cardstocks

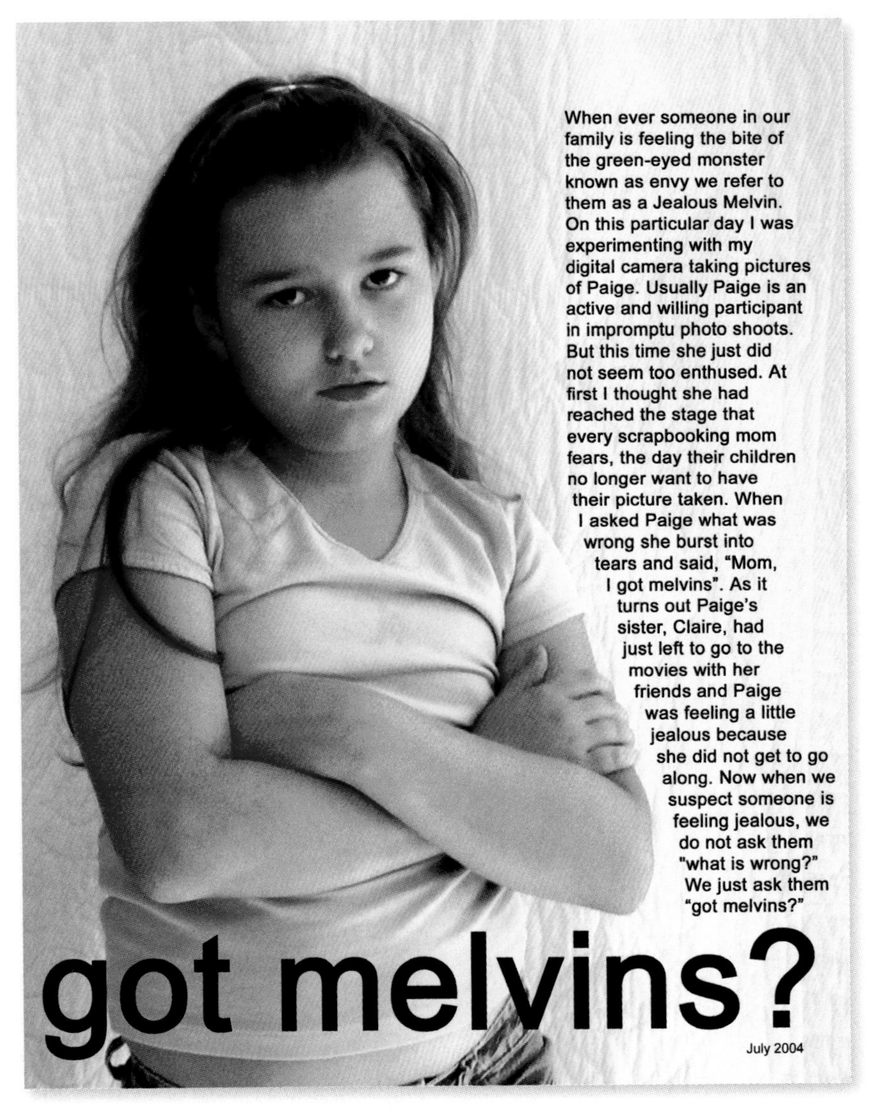

Is there a secret phrase or word you use in your household to communicate a feeling or emotion? If you don't mind letting the cat out of the bag, your scrapbook pages are a great place to feature these one-of-kind conversations. It will serve as a great way to remember silly speech years down the road, and future generations who keep the tradition alive will know how it got started.

Families often transform sayings or phrases into their own special communications. Julie designed this page showcasing a family phrase, "Got Melvins?" that came into being during an impromptu photo shoot and a conversation with her daughter. She featured one of the photos from the shoot and told the entire story in her journaling.

SUPPLIES: Image-editing software (Adobe Photoshop Elements)

Before You - *Melodee Langworthy, Rockford, Michigan*

Take a stab writing your own heartfelt sentiments in poetic form. Don't get discouraged if you find this form of writing is a challenge. Even the greatest poets reworked their writing to achieve the perfect structure and flow. The best advice for beginners is to not worry about meter or rhyme but instead focus on the feelings you are trying to convey. Craft your words so the meaning carries the greatest weight.

When Melodee captured this moment between her husband and son on film, she wanted to put the emotions on paper. She wrote a poem and created the layout to share those feelings and preserve them for years. For others thinking about writing poetry, she says, "Take advantage of those moments when something really strikes your heart, and write your emotions on paper as soon as you can. That is when my journaling really has life in it."

SUPPLIES: Patterned papers, die-cut word blocks (My Mind's Eye); twill (Scenic Route Paper Co.); letter and phrase stickers (Mustard Moon, Sweetwater, Wordsworth); chalk ink (Clearsnap)

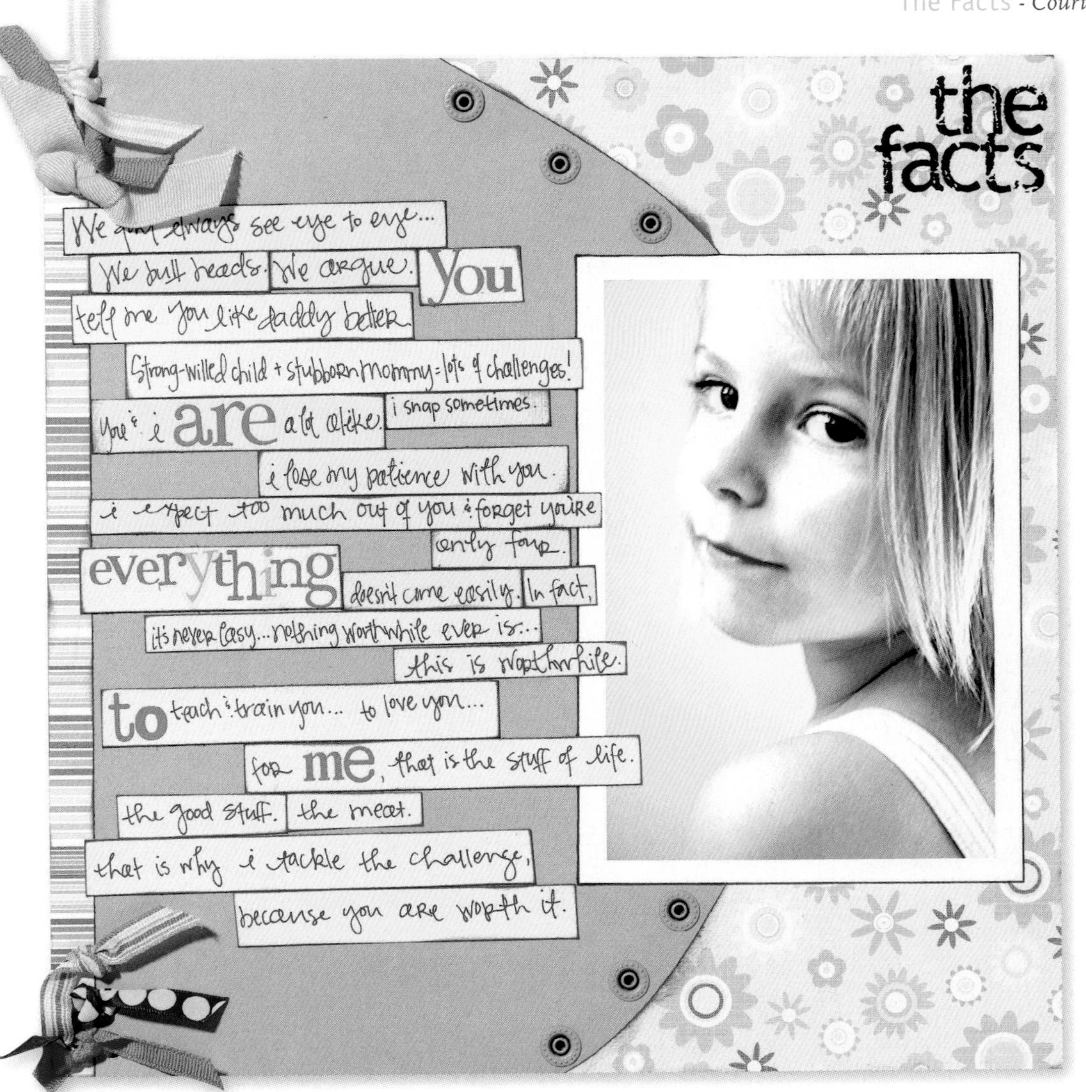

Secret-message journaling is a clever technique that requires just a little bit of planning. Draft your secret message first. Then compose your supporting text around the secret message. Contrast the secret message with the supporting text by using a different font, color or type of lettering so that the secret message pops and is visible to your readers.

Courtney journaled about the struggles she faces being a mom. Highlighted within the text, however, is an overall message of love. She used cardstock strips with handwritten journaling to carry her thoughts. To highlight a sentence within the text, she used green rub-on letters to create each of the words. Her choice of bold colors and whimsical ribbons and papers reinforces the mood of the photo.

Supplies: Patterned papers, ribbons, rivets (Chatterbox); rub-on letters (Paper House Productions); watermark ink (Tsukineko); letter stickers (Anna Griffin); stamping ink; pen; cardstocks

ADDITIONAL CREDITS & SUPPLIES

Page 3 What About the Words?

In this page, Amy employed the letter-writing format of journaling to introduce the concept of the book to readers. Pretty paisleys, paper flowers and a metal embellishment tucked in the lower right corner lend an air of femininity and grace.

Amy Glander, Memory Makers Books
Photo: Ken Trujillo, Memory Makers Books

Supplies: Patterned paper (Chatterbox); paper flowers (Prima); die-cut letters (QuicKutz); "?" sticker (Creative Imaginations); metal embellishment, mini brads (Making Memories); cardstocks

Page 7 Everything Goes Better With a Friend

Amy created this page using a play on words from a popular soda pop advertisement. Her title font mimics the label's trademark shape. Aligning the word "time," she added a vertical column of journaling. Amy cropped four photos the same size and used them as a border along the bottom, highlighting several with acrylic letters that she adhered upside down and one with an acrylic frame.

Amy Goldstein, Kent Lakes, New York

Supplies: Patterned paper, cotton art tape, coasters (Imagination Project); acrylic frame (Making Memories); metal-rimmed tag (American Crafts); acrylic word charm (KI Memories); acrylic word (Junkitz); circle punch; cardstock

Page 23 Pockets of Wisdom

Inspired by patterned paper that featured a number of quotes, Franny created this page for her son. She trimmed and tucked the quotes into self-adhesive fabric pockets. With the addition of an Irish blessing, she hopes he will understand that she wants the best for him. The warm-colored papers and embellishments make the black-and-white photo pop off the page.

Franny Lesniak, Pflugerville, Texas

Supplies: Patterned papers, rivets (Chatterbox); letter stamps (FontWerks, PSX Design); letter stickers (EK Success); fabric pockets, leather flower (Making Memories); phrase strips (K & Company); ribbon (May Arts); paper clips (Boxer Scrapbook Productions); chipboard monogram, clipboard clip (Karen Foster Design); stamping inks; cardstocks

Page 49 Four

Favorites seem abundant when you turn 4. Angelia interviewed her daughter to discover hers. She transcribed the conversation across the top half of the page and added pearl buttons, paper flowers and stitching. She used muted pink tones along with soft whites to keep the page dainty and feminine.

Angelia Wigginton, Belmont, Mississippi

Supplies: Patterned papers, stencil letter (Autumn Leaves); textured cardstock (Bazzill); paper flowers, definition sticker, rub-on letters (Making Memories); flower buttons (SEI); photo corners (Canson); metal photo corners (source unknown); vellum; brads; lace; flower buttons; pearl beads

Page 71 Senses

Jodi's vibrant photo encapsulates the sunny warmth reflecting off the hibiscus. Using the five senses as her blueprint, she captured each sensation in journaling blocks matted on brown cardstock.

Jodi Amidei, Memory Makers Books

Supplies: Patterned paper (Anna Griffin, Carolee's Creations); die-cut letters (QuicKutz); cardstock

SOURCE GUIDE

The following companies manufacture products featured in this book. Please check your local retailers to find these materials, or go to a company's Web site for the latest product. In addition, we have made every attempt to properly credit the items mentioned in this book. We apologize to any company that we have listed incorrectly, and we would appreciate hearing from you.

3L Corp.
(800) 828-3130
www.scrapbook-adhesives.com

3M
(800) 364-3577
www.3m.com

7 Gypsies
(877) 749-7797
www.sevengypsies.com

Accu-Cut®
(800) 288-1670
www.accucut.com

Adobe Systems Incorporated
(866) 766-2256
www.adobe.com

All My Memories
(888) 553-1998
www.allmymemories.com

Altered Book Club, The
(888) 85-ALTER
www.alteredbookclub.com

American Crafts
(801) 226-0747
www.americancrafts.com

American Traditional Designs®
(800) 448-6656
www.americantraditional.com

Anima Designs
(800) 570-6847
www.animadesigns.com

Anna Griffin, Inc.
(888) 817-8170
www.annagriffin.com

ArcSoft®, Inc.
(510) 440-9901
www.arcsoft.com

Autumn Leaves
(800) 588-6707
www.autumnleaves.com

Basic Grey™
(801) 451-6006
www.basicgrey.com

Bazzill Basics Paper
(480) 558-8557
www.bazzillbasics.com

Berwick Offray, LLC
(800) 344-5533
www.offray.com

Blue Moon Beads
(800) 377-6715
www.bluemoonbeads.com

Bo-Bunny Press
(801) 771-4010
www.bobunny.com

Boxer Scrapbook Productions
(503) 625-0455
www.boxerscrapbooks.com

Broderbund Software
(319) 247-3325
www.broderbund.com

C & T Publishing
(800) 284-1114
www.ctpub.com

Canson®, Inc.
(800) 628-9283
www.canson-us.com

CARL Mfg. USA, Inc.
(800) 257-4771
www.carl-products.com

Carolee's Creations®
(435) 563-1100
www.ccpaper.com

Chatterbox, Inc.
(208) 939-9133
www.chatterboxinc.com

Clearsnap, Inc.
(360) 293-6634
www.clearsnap.com

Clipiola- no contact info

Close To My Heart®
(888) 655-6552
www.closetomyheart.com

Coats & Clark
(800) 648-1479
www.coatsandclark.com

Colorbök™, Inc.
(800) 366-4660
www.colorbok.com

Crafty Secrets Publications
(888) 597-8898
www.craftysecrets.com

Creative Imaginations
(800) 942-6487
www.cigift.com

Creative Impressions Rubber Stamps, Inc.
(719) 596-4860
www.creativeimpressions.com

Creative Memories®
(800) 468-9335
www.creativememories.com

Cross-My Heart-Cards, Inc.
(888) 689-8808
www.crossmyheart.com

Daisy D's Paper Company
(888) 601-8955
www.daisydspaper.com

Darice, Inc.
(800_ 321-1494
www.darice.com

Dèjá Views
(800) 243-8419
www.dejaviews.com

Delta Technical Coatings, Inc.
(800) 423-4135
www.deltacrafts.com

Deluxe Designs
(480) 497-9005
www.deluxedesigns.com

Destination™ Scrapbook Designs
(866) 806-7826
www.destinationstickers.com

DieCuts with a View™
(877) 221-6107
www.dcwv.com

DMC Corp.
(973) 589-0606
www.dmc.com

DMD Industries, Inc.
(800) 805-9890
www.dmdind.com

Doodlebug Design™ Inc.
(801) 966-9952
www.doodlebug.ws

Dymo
(800) 426-7827
www.dymo.com

EK Success™, Ltd.
(800) 524-1349
www.eksuccess.com

Emagination Crafts, Inc.
(866) 238-9770
www.emaginationcrafts.com

Everlasting Keepsakes™ by faith
(816) 896-7037
www.everlastinkeepsakes.com

Fiber Scraps™
(215) 230-4905
www.fiberscraps.com

Fiskars®, Inc.
(800) 950-0203
www.fiskars.com

Flair® Designs
(888) 546-9990
www.flairdesignsinc.com

FontWerks
(604) 942-3105
www.fontwerks.com

FoofaLa
(402) 330-3208
www.foofala.com

Foundations- no contact info

Go West Studios
(214) 227-0007
www.goweststudios.com

Heidi Swapp/Advantus Corporation
(904) 482-0092
www.heidiswapp.com

Hero Arts® Rubber Stamps, Inc.
(800) 822-4376
www.heroarts.com

Hobby Lobby Stores, Inc.
www.hobbylobby.com

Hot Off The Press, Inc.
(800) 227-9595
www.paperpizazz.com

Imagination Project, Inc.
(513) 860-2711
www.imaginationproject.com

International Spy Museum
(877) SPY-BUYS
www.spymuseumstore.com

Jesse James & Co., Inc.
(610) 435-0201
www.jessejamesbutton.com

JewelCraft, LLC
(201) 223-0804
www.jewelcraft.biz

Jo-Ann Stores
(888) 739-4120
www.joann.com

JudiKins
(310) 515-1115
www.judikins.com

Junkitz™
(732) 792-1108
www.junkitz.com

K & Company
(888) 244-2083
www.kandcompany.com

Karen Foster Design
(801) 451-9779
www.karenfosterdesign.com

KI Memories
(972) 243-5595
www.kimemories.com

Krylon®
(216) 566-200
www.krylon.com

La Pluma, Inc.
(803) 749-4076
www.debrabeagle.com

Li'l Davis Designs
(949) 838-0344
www.lildavisdesigns.com

Lion Brand Yarn Company
www.lionbrand.com

M & J Trimming
(800) 9-MJTRIM
www.mjtrim.com

Magenta Rubber Stamps
(800) 565-5254
www.magentastyle.com

Magic Scraps™
(972) 238-1838
www.magicscraps.com

Making Memories
(800) 286-5263
www.makingmemories.com

Mara-Mi, Inc.
(800) 627-2648
www.mara-mi.com

Marvy® Uchida/ Uchida of America, Corp.
(800) 541-5877
www.uchida.com

May Arts
(800) 442-3950
www.mayarts.com

McGill, Inc.
(800) 982-9884
www.mcgillinc.com

me & my BiG ideas®
(949) 883-2065
www.meandmybigideas.com

Memories Complete™, LLC
(866) 966-6365
www.memoriescomplete.com

Memories In Uniform
(757) 228-7395
www.memoriesinuniform.com

Michaels® Arts & Crafts
(800) 642-4235
www.michaels.com

Microsoft Corporation
www.microsoft.com

Midori
(800) 659-3049
www.midoriribbon.com

Morex Corporation
(717) 852-7771
www.morexcorp.com

Mrs. Grossman's Paper Company
(800) 429-4549
www.mrsgrossmans.com

Mustard Moon™
(408) 299-8542
www.mustardmoon.com

My Mind's Eye™, Inc.
(800) 665-5116
www.frame-ups.com

NRN Designs
(800) 421-6958
www.nrndesigns.com

nuART Handmade Papers
(630) 881-1595
www.nuartpapers.com

Nunn Design
(360) 379-3557
www.nunndesign.com

Office Max
www.officemax.com

Offray- see Berwick Offray, LLC

On The Surface
(847) 675-2520

Outlines™ Rubber Stamp Company, Inc.
(860) 228-3686
www.outlinesrubberstamp.com

Oxford- no contact info

Paperbilities- no contact info

Paper House Productions®
(800) 255-7316
www.paperhouseproductions.com

Paper Loft
(866) 254-1961
www.paperloft.com

Paper Studio- no contact info

Pebbles Inc.
(801) 224-1857
www.pebblesinc.com

Pioneer Photo Albums, Inc.®
(800) 366-3686
www.pioneerphotoalbums.com

Plaid Enterprises, Inc.
(800) 842-4197
www.plaidonline.com

Prima Marketing, Inc.
(909) 627-5532
www.mulberrypaperflowers.com

Provo Craft®
(888) 577-3545
www.provocraft.com

PSX Design™
(800) 782-6748
www.psxdesign.com

Punch Bunch, The
(254) 791-4209
www.thepunchbunch.com

Queen & Co.
(858) 485-5132
www.queenandcompany.com

QuicKutz, Inc.
(801) 765-1144
www.quickutz.com

Rand McNally
www.randmcnally.com

Ranger Industries, Inc.
(800) 244-2211
www.rangerink.com

Reminisce Papers
(319) 358-9777
www.shopreminisce.com

Rubber Cottage
(330) 722-2863
www.rubbercottage.com

Rusty Pickle
(801) 746-1045
www.rustypickle.com

S.R.M. Press, Inc.
(800) 323-9589
www.srmpress.com

Sandylion Sticker Designs
(800) 387-4215
www.sandylion.com

Sanford® Corporation
(800) 323-0749
www.sanfordcorp.com

Savvy Stamps
(866) 44-SAVVY
www.savvystamps.com

Scenic Route Paper Co.
(801) 785-0761
www.scenicroutepaper.com

Scissor Sisters
(877) PRESSTO
www.scissor-sisters.com

ScrapArts
(503) 631-4893
www.scraparts.com

Scrapbook Wizard™, The
(435) 752-7555
www.scrapbookwizard.com

Scraptivity™ Scrapbooking, Inc.
(800) 393-2151
www.scraptivity.com

Scrapworks, LLC
(801) 363-1010
www.scrapworks.com

SEI, Inc.
(800) 333-3279
www.shopsei.com

Sizzix®
(866) 742-4447
www.sizzix.com

Stamp Craft- see Plaid Enterprises

Stampin' Up!®
(800) 782-6787
www.stampinup.com

Stampington & Company
(877) STAMPER
www.stampington.com

Stampotique
(602) 862-0237
www.stampotique.com

Sticker Studio™
(208) 322-2465
www.stickerstudio.com

Sweetwater
(800) 359-3094
www.sweetwaterscrapbook.com

Target
www.target.com

Timeless Touches™/Dove Valley Productions, LLC
(623) 362-8285
www.timelesstouches.net

Tsukineko®, Inc.
(800) 769-6633
www.tsukineko.com

Urban Lily- no contact info

Wal-Mart Stores, Inc.
(800) WALMART
www.walmart.com

Weathered Door, The- no contact info

Weberley & Friends™/Paper Island Greetings
www.weberley.com

Walnut Hollow® Farm, Inc.
(800) 950-5101
www.walnuthollow.com

Wendi Speciale Designs
www.wendispeciale.com

Westrim® Crafts
(800) 727-2727
www.westrimcrafts.com

Wishblade™, Inc.
(651) 644-5144
www.wishblade.com

Wordsworth
(719) 282-3495
www.wordsworthstamps.com

Wrights® Ribbon Accents
(877) 597-4448
www.wrights.com

INDEX

Learn more from these fine titles from Memory Makers Books!

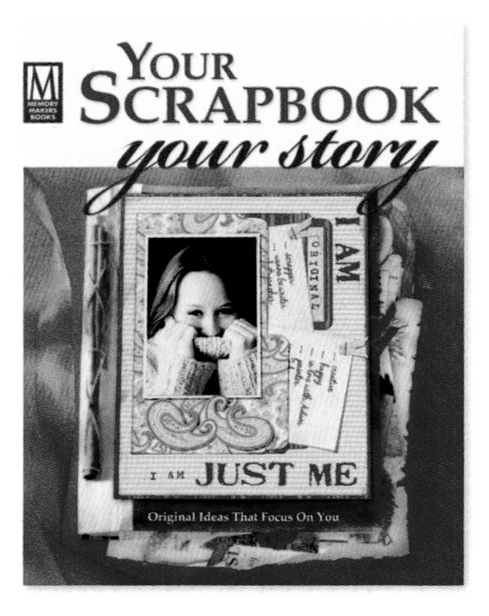

Your Scrapbook Your Story
ISBN-13 978-1-892127-60-0
ISBN-10 1-892127-60-1
Paperback
112 pgs.
#33437

Scrapbooking Family Memories
ISBN-13 978-1-892127-59-4
ISBN-10 1-892127-59-8
Paperback
128 pgs.
#33439

Scrapbook Journaling Made Simle
ISBN-13 978-1-892127-23-5
ISBN-10 1-892127-23-7
Paperback
96 pgs.
#32459

Scrapbook Lettering
ISBN-13 978-1-892127-15-0
ISBN-10 1-892127-15-6
Paperback
112 pgs.
#32682

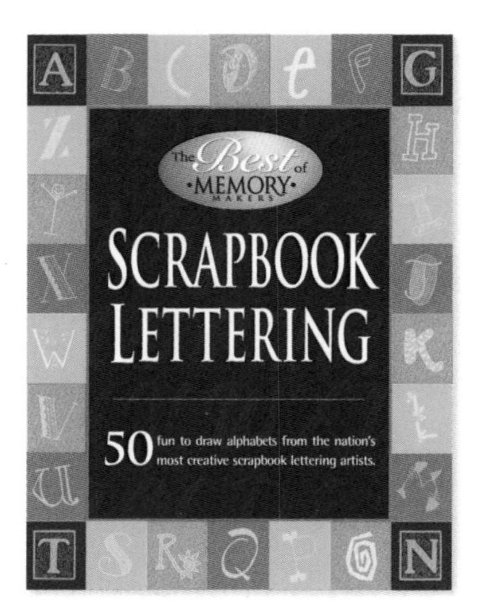

These books and other fine Memory Makers Books titles are available from your local art or craft retailer, bookstore or online supplier. Please see page 2 of this book for contact information for Canada, Australia, the U.K. and Europe.